well bred • well fed • well hung

how to buy & cook real meat

C000050596

well bred • well fed • well hung
how to buy & cook real meat

Antony Worrall Thompson

Little Books by Big Names™

*Special thanks to David Wilby and
the team at Notting Grill*

First published in the United Kingdom in 2003 by Little Books Ltd,
48 Catherine Place, London SW1E 6HL

10 9 8 7 6 5 4 3 2 1

A CIP catalogue record for this book is available from the British Library.

ISBN: 1 904435 08 4

*Many thanks to: Jamie Ambrose for editorial management,
Gray Jolliffe for illustrations, Mousemat Design for jacket and text design,
Margaret Campbell of Scan-Hi Digital and Craig Campbell of QSP Print
for printing consultancy, and Ann Barrett for indexing.
Printed and bound in Scotland by Scotprint.*

CONTENTS

INTRODUCTION

Meat is back on the menu. For about ten years we've hidden our meat-eating needs in the closet, aware that BSE and foot-and-mouth disease made eating and discussing the product politically incorrect. It was a time for animal-rights activists and hard-core veggies to shout the loudest and work on our insecurities. Yet this has been a short-lived exercise. Over the last few years, 600,000 vegetarians have deserted the cause and secretly begun chewing the bone. Welcome back.

Certainly, BSE was caused by intensive farming, stemming either from supermarkets' desire to supply us with cheap meat or the public demanding it. This book is not about encouraging you to eat more meat; it's about asking you to be more selective, to care about an animal's welfare, to want to know where and how it lived, to eat it a little less often, but when you do, to spend more and buy the best.

In many ways, I encourage the Indian diet where vegetables make up the bulk of the week's diet and meat is eaten on special occasions. So when you buy that £2.99 chicken, be aware of its miserable 40-day existence sharing a square metre of barn with eight other chickens, its diet possibly laden with antibiotics and growth enhancers. Ignore that bright-red piece of beef with its pristine white fat in the knowledge that it will have been killed about five days earlier and will have no flavour, will be flabby with blood, and won't have aged enough to be tender. Don't be tempted by that fat-free pork look-alike that is a mere shadow of the real thing; seek out some rare breeds from a specialist butcher. Once you've tasted Middle White, Gloucester Old Spot or one of the other rare breeds, you'll never return to the dry, cardboard-tasting reproduction.

To be fair, lamb is the one meat that has escaped most of the flak. It feeds on pastures and has a fairly normal existence, but you can still broaden your meat-scape by looking for named varieties such as Herdwick or Suffolk or a breed that feeds on salt marsh or herb-filled pastures.

So enjoy your meat, but be more selective and, where possible, buy British. The meat crisis appears to be over. We are producing excellent meat. Now all we need to do is up the ante and pay more attention to our traditional breeds.

1
Chicken

BUYING CHICKEN

What a state our chicken industry is in. The United Kingdom is meant to be a first-world country, and yet a large percentage of all chickens reared in the UK still carry the salmonella or campilobacter bacteria – which is a disgrace. One colleague in the industry, well-known for his salads and sandwiches, has had to import chickens from Spain just to guarantee serving a salmonella-free product.

The problem lies with the farmers and intensive farming, where incorrect feeds are all aimed at producing a cheaper bird for the consumer. In many ways, the way intensively farmed chickens are reared is criminal: such little space, little ability to move, reduced ventilation, increased feeding on an unnatural high-protein meat and fish diet. Is it surprising that they get diseases? And yet we continue to go into our supermarkets time after time to buy our cheap chicken. If only the public were prepared to pay a little more, these problems would eventually disappear.

Chicken is one of the biggest cons in the meat market. It comes over all innocent as the meat to trust; low in saturated fat, it appears to be the healthy option. Don't be fooled. Cheap chicken is not for you – unless, of course, you're happy eating a bird that has been fattened on growth enhancers and antibiotics – and that's forgetting that the poor birds have a life span of about forty days, are often forced to have their beaks trimmed, and are made to grow breasts so large their legs won't support them. And then there is the possibility that soon they may be bred without feathers to make them even cheaper to 'harvest'. It's your choice.

Many years ago, when I was a boy, it was a real treat to have a roast chicken, but now it is commonplace. Funny how life goes full circle. In those days, the cheap white meat (apart from pork) was rabbit, which is now three times as expensive as chicken. Today we get bored with chickens in restaurants, but look forward to an interesting rabbit dish.

When you go to buy chicken, always check the labels attached to any packaging. They can be broken down into five categories.

Corn-fed

These chickens have yellow flesh and are fed on a diet of at least seventy percent corn, maize or cereal, but do not be fooled: they will almost certainly have not seen the light of day, being barn-reared. They are not likely to have any more flavour than the birds in the next category.

Intensively reared

These are birds that are, when all is said and done, battery-farmed chickens with a short, uncomfortable life.

Free-range barn

A little better but still to be avoided, if at all possible. The birds are free to move about inside barns, but are often housed two deep, with regular fighting among the inmates. The average 1.5kg birds, battery- or barn-reared, are about forty days old when they reach the supermarkets.

Traditional free-range

The birds are less intensively reared, are at least eighty-one days old and have access to grass.

Organic free-range

We must encourage the buying of organic free-range birds. In feather, they may look a little rough-and-ready, and they may be a little tougher, but this is more than made up for in their flavour. Plus the big bonus is 'they have had a life'. Organic always means the birds will have been reared free-range and fed on a certfied organic diet.

THAI GREEN CHICKEN CURRY

I am really into this smooth, silky curry. It's also very easy to make. Green curry paste is now available in supermarkets, but better versions can be found in most Asian stores.

Serves 4
1-2 tbsp green curry paste
30ml or 1 fl oz vegetable oil
1 tsp garlic, mashed with a little salt
2 stalks lemon grass, tender part only,
*   finely chopped*
2 lime leaves, shredded
750ml or 27 fl oz coconut milk
12 chicken thighs, skin removed
2-3 green chillies, deseeded, finely chopped
4 tbsp chopped coriander leaves and
*   tender stalks*
4 tbsp ripped basil leaves
juice of 2 limes
30ml or 1 fl oz Thai fish sauce (nam pla)

1 Fry the curry paste in the vegetable oil over a high heat for 3 minutes. Add the garlic, lemon grass, lime leaves and half the coconut milk and cook until the sauce starts to split – about 5 minutes.

2 Add the chicken thighs, chillies and coriander and simmer for 10 minutes. Add the remaining coconut milk and cook for a further 5 minutes.

3 Just before serving, fold in the basil leaves, lime juice and fish sauce. Serve with fragrant rice and garnish with coriander leaves.

Classic roast chicken

You can give me all the poncy chicken dishes in the world, but I'll always come back to this great old classic. The roast chicken, as long as it's ideally organic but definitely free-range, is a top-dollar bird.

Serves 4
1 large, free-range chicken
    (about 1.5kg or 3 lb 5 oz)
55g or 2 oz softened unsalted butter
1 tsp sea salt
several grindings of black pepper
½ lemon
2 sprigs thyme
1 small onion, cut in half
1 head garlic, broken into cloves
175ml or 6 fl oz dry white wine
300ml or 10 fl oz chicken stock
1 tsp anchovy essence
ground white pepper

METHOD

1 Preheat the oven to 230°C or 450°F or gas mark 8.

2 Rub the chicken with half the butter, sprinkle with the sea salt and black pepper. Pop the lemon, thyme and onion into the chicken's cavity. Put into a roasting tray with the garlic cloves, white wine and half the stock. Roast for 20 minutes.

3 Reduce the heat to 190°C (375°F, gas mark 5) and roast for 45 minutes more, basting from time to time. Turn off the oven, place the chicken on a carving dish and return to the oven to rest for 10 to 15 minutes before carving.

4 Place the chicken roasting dish over a low flame to make the gravy. Mash the garlic cloves with the back of a fork into the roasting juices.

5 Pour in the remaining chicken stock and scrape any coagulated juices from the bottom of the pan. Add the anchovy essence and a few grindings of white pepper; stir to combine. Taste; if the flavour is too strong, add a little water. The gravy will be quite fatty, but that's its beauty: pure heaven created from the cooking juices.

6 Pour any juices from the relaxing chicken into the gravy. Strain the gravy into a jug or gravy boat.

7 For a thicker gravy, cook 25g (1 oz) each butter and flour for 5 minutes over a low heat. Add the cooking juices little by little until you get the required thickness. Cook about 15 minutes to remove any floury taste, strain, then use immediately.

Southern fried chicken

I couldn't write a chicken chapter without including this recipe. It's deeply unfashionable but who cares? Whenever I eat it, I love it.

Serves 4
600ml or 20 fl oz buttermilk or single cream
6 tbsp chopped coriander leaves
6 garlic cloves, finely chopped
2 shallots, finely chopped
½ tbsp dried chilli flakes
1 tbsp salt
4 large chicken breasts, skin removed
6 tbsp plain flour
½ tsp celery salt
½ tsp cayenne pepper
½ tsp freshly ground black pepper
½ tsp paprika
vegetable oil, for frying

1 Combine the buttermilk or cream with the coriander, garlic, shallots, chilli flakes and salt. Pour over the chicken breasts, cover, and marinate overnight in the fridge.

2 Combine the flour with the celery salt, cayenne pepper, black pepper and paprika. Lift the chicken breasts from the marinade and dip them in the seasoned flour to coat. Place them in the refrigerator for 45 minutes.

3 Fill a frying pan with 1cm (half an inch) of oil. Fry the chicken breasts in the hot oil for 10 minutes each side, or until thoroughly cooked and golden.

Pot-roasted chicken with
tarragon & baked apples

Serves 4
25g or 1 oz unsalted butter
1 tbsp olive oil
1 fresh chicken,
*   about 1.5kg or 3 lb 4 oz*
salt and pepper, to taste
1 onion, finely chopped
1 stick celery, roughly chopped
1 carrot, roughly chopped
115g or 4 oz bacon lardons
1 bay leaf
1 sprig thyme
1 Bramley apple, peeled, cored, cut into
*   large chunks*
300ml or 10 fl oz chicken stock
450ml or 16 fl oz dry white wine
300ml or 10 fl oz double cream
4 tbsp flat-leaf parsley, chopped
1 tbsp tarragon, chopped

For the baked apples
4 small apples, cored
1 packet of your favourite stuffing, made ahead
25g or 1 oz softened butter
1 tbsp soft, light-brown sugar

To garnish
4 slices crispy pancetta or smoked streaky bacon
new potatoes

1 Preheat the oven to 190°C or 375°F or gas mark 5.

2 Remove about 2.5cm (1 inch) diameter of core from the apples, leaving 5mm (¼-inch) uncut at the bottom. Run the tip of a sharp knife around the outside of the apple, just to pierce the skin. This stops them bursting in the oven. Spoon the stuffing into the apple cavities.

3 Place the apples onto a baking tray that has been brushed with a little butter, dot the tops with a little extra butter and brown sugar and bake in the oven for about half an hour, basting a few times during cooking; keep warm.

4 Meanwhile, melt the butter in a large, non-stick casserole pot and add the olive oil to prevent burning. Season the chicken with salt and freshly ground black pepper, and place it into the casserole pot. Brown until pale golden on all sides. Remove from the pot and set aside.

5 Add the onions, celery, carrot and bacon and cook until the bacon is crispy and the onions have softened – about 10 minutes. Reduce the heat and add the bay leaf and thyme.

6 Return the chicken to the pot and sprinkle with the chopped apples. Add half the stock and half the white wine. Bring to a gentle simmer, cover and place in the oven for about 45 minutes.

7 Remove the chicken from the pot and place on a chopping board. Remove the legs, wings and breasts and set aside to keep warm. Chop the carcass into four pieces and place back into the pot with the vegetables and the remaining white wine and stock. Bring to a boil and simmer gently for 15 minutes.

8 Strain the sauce into a bowl through a fine-meshed sieve. Pour the strained sauce back into the pot. Reduce by half. Add the cream and simmer for a further 5 minutes, or until the sauce is creamy and slightly thickened. Fold in the parsley and tarragon. Season to taste.

9 Return the chicken pieces to the pot to warm through and become coated in the sauce. Remove the apples from the oven.

10 Serve on a warm serving plate. Pour a little of the sauce over the meat, place a baked apple to the side of the chicken and garnish with crispy pancetta and new potatoes.

BANG-BANG CHICKEN

Made popular in western circles at Le Caprice restaurant in London and now copied everywhere – but surprisingly, in very few Oriental restaurants. Some cooks make it with a sesame sauce; I prefer a peanut one.

Serves 6
1 really useful poached 1.5kg or 3 lb 5 oz chicken (see page 28)
125g or 4½ oz Chinese glass noodles
4 garlic cloves, peeled and lightly smashed
1 bunch coriander, roughly chopped
175g or 6 oz smooth peanut butter
4 tbsp light soy sauce
2 tbsp runny honey
1 tsp chilli oil
2 tbsp Japanese rice vinegar
1 tbsp dry sherry
2 cucumbers, peeled, deseeded, cut in thin strips

1 Remove the skin and any bones from the chicken and beat it with a rolling pin to loosen the fibres. Shred the meat with a knife or pull it apart with two forks. Set aside.

2 Soak the noodles in boiling water for 1 minute. Separate and drain.

3 Blend the garlic in a food processor until finely chopped, add the coriander and blend again until fairly smooth. Add the peanut butter, soy sauce, honey, chilli oil, vinegar and sherry and blend until smooth. If it looks too thick, add a little water.

4 Spread a pile of noodles in the centre of six plates. Top with the cucumber strips, then the chicken. Drizzle with the peanut sauce, but do not smother it. Garnish with extra coriander leaves. Serve any remaining sauce separately.

THE REALLY USEFUL
CHICKEN RECIPE

This poached chicken recipe has a myriad of uses in chicken curries, sandwiches, salads, in Bang-bang Chicken (page 26), or just as it is served with a soy dip.

Serves 4
1 x 1.5kg or 3 lb 5 oz free-range chicken
1 litre or 35 fl oz chicken stock
4 spring onions, sliced
115g or 4 oz fresh ginger, cut into thin discs
6 garlic cloves, peeled
2 whole red chillies
1 tbsp sea salt
1 tsp peppercorns

1 Place the chicken in a tightly fitting saucepan. Pour in the stock and top up with water so that only 5cm (2 inches) of chicken is visible. Add the remaining ingredients.

2 Bring to the boil, cover and simmer for 25 minutes, turning the chicken once during the cooking process.

3 Keep covered and switch off the heat. Allow the chicken to relax in the liquor for 1 hour. Remove and leave until cool, then refrigerate until ready for use. The cooking liquor makes an excellent stock for chicken soup.

TERIYAKI CHICKEN THIGHS WITH ROAST GARLIC NOODLES

Serves 4
5 tbsp dark soy sauce
3 tbsp Mirin or dry sherry
3 tbsp soft brown sugar
2 tbsp grated fresh ginger
2 garlic cloves, finely chopped
12 skinned and boned chicken thighs
1 bulb garlic
3 tbsp olive oil
4 spring onions, finely chopped
1 tsp soft thyme leaves
280g or 10 oz dried egg-noodles
85g or 3 oz baby spinach leaves
salt and freshly ground black pepper

1 Combine the soy sauce, Mirin, sugar, ginger and garlic in a shallow dish. Add the chicken thighs, cover, and refrigerate overnight or for 2 hours, turning from time to time.

2 Cut 5mm (¼ inch) from the top of the garlic bulb and dribble the cut edge of the cloves with 1 teaspoon of the olive oil. Wrap in foil and roast at 190°C (375°F or gas mark 5) for about 30 minutes, until the garlic appears soft.

3 Squeeze the garlic cloves from their skins into a frying pan. Add the remaining oil, onions and thyme. Cook over a moderate heat until the onions are soft but not coloured.

4 Cook the noodles according to the packet instructions; drain. Tip into the garlic and onion mixture; toss. Fold in the spinach leaves and toss until the leaves have wilted. Season to taste.

5 Preheat the grill. Cook the chicken thighs for 6 minutes each side, basting with the marinade several times. Serve immediately on the noodles.

ORIENTAL CHICKEN WINGS

Serves 4-6
1 tbsp Szechuan peppercorns, toasted and
    ground in a coffee grinder
1 tbsp garlic, minced
3 tbsp fresh ginger, minced
4 tbsp orange zest, finely grated
    (reserve 1 tbsp for garnish)
8 spring onions, finely sliced
1 hot chilli, finely chopped
2 tbsp liquid honey
2 tbsp soy sauce
300ml or 10 fl oz corn oil
125ml or 4 fl oz sesame oil
salt and freshly ground black pepper
1kg or 2 lb 2 oz chicken wings, cut in half
    through the joint, tips discarded
2 tbsp chopped coriander
2 tbsp snipped chives

1 With a pestle and mortar, mash together the Szechuan peppercorns, garlic, ginger, orange zest, half the spring onions and chilli until you have a paste.

2 In a large bowl combine the honey, the soy sauce and oils with the paste. Season to taste. Add the chicken wings and allow them to marinate for at least 4 hours, or preferably overnight.

3 Cook on a hot barbecue for 7 to 8 minutes each side, or until the chicken is thoroughly cooked and dark golden-brown.

4 Garnish with a mixture of the reserved orange zest, remaining spring onions, chopped coriander and chives.

Stracciatella
ITALIAN CHICKEN SOUP

Serves 2
600ml or 20 fl oz good chicken stock
1 glass red wine
2 eggs
2 tbsp freshly grated Parmesan
2 tbsp chopped parsley
1 tbsp snipped chives
grated nutmeg
salt and freshly ground black pepper

1 Bring the chicken stock to the boil. Add the red wine and return to the boil.

2 In a bowl, beat together the eggs, Parmesan, parsley, chives, and a good pinch of nutmeg.

3 Pour this mixture into the hot broth in a continuous stream, stirring with a fork. Cook undisturbed for another minute until the eggs are set.

4 It will have a raggedy look, but don't worry – it tastes delicious. Season to taste.

CHICKEN NOODLE SOUP

Sad person that I am, I used to enjoy chicken noodle soup from a packet – that is, until I discovered this Vietnamese recipe.

Serves 6
1 x 1.5kg or 3 lb 5 oz free-range chicken
3 litres or 5¼ pints chicken stock
2 tsp salt
1 x 2.5cm or 1-inch piece of ginger,
    peeled and sliced
2 garlic cloves
4 tbsp Thai fish sauce (nam pla)
10 black peppercorns
2 onions, peeled and finely sliced
4 tbsp crisp-fried shallots (available from
    Chinese supermarkets)
300g or 10 oz rice noodles
6 spring onions, sliced
3 tbsp chopped coriander

1 Pop the chicken into a large pot. Cover with the stock and add the salt, ginger, garlic, fish sauce, peppercorns, onions and shallots. Bring to the boil, reduce the heat and simmer for 30 minutes. Remove the chicken and set aside.

2 Continue simmering for another 1½ hours to reduce the stock by half. Strain, and return to the heat. Skim off any fat.

3 Break the noodles into 2.5cm (1-inch) pieces into a large bowl and cover with boiling water. Leave 1 minute, then drain.

4 Slice or dice the chicken and return to the stock. Put the noodles into a soup tureen or six bowls and top with the chicken and broth. Sprinkle on the spring onions and coriander.

5 Serve with lime wedges, thinly sliced red chillies and sprigs of basil.

Roast turkey with parsley, thyme and bacon stuffing

Serves 4
115g or 4 oz ricotta or cream cheese
115g or 4 oz unsalted butter, softened
1 tbsp snipped chives
1 tbsp chopped flat-leaf parsley
2 tsp chopped tarragon
1 tsp chopped chervil
½ tsp freshly ground black pepper
¼ tsp sea salt
1 x 4.5kgs (10 lb) fresh turkey, at
    room temperature
½ lemon
½ onion
3 garlic cloves
1 sprig thyme
1 sprig rosemary
extra butter, for greasing foil
3 onions, peeled and cut in chunks
12 bay leaves
600ml or 20 fl oz chicken stock

For the stuffing
1 tbsp olive oil
115g or 4 oz smoked bacon or pancetta,
    cut into small (2.5cm or 1-inch) pieces
1 onion, finely diced
1 stick celery, finely sliced
1 packet parsley and thyme stuffing
55g or 2 oz melted butter
2 tsp grated lemon rind

For the gravy
150ml or 5 fl oz red wine
1 tbsp redcurrant jelly
1 tbsp cornflour
salt and freshly ground black pepper

METHOD

1 Combine the ricotta and butter with the chopped herbs, salt and pepper.

2 Gently ease the skin sway from the flesh at both ends of the turkey by carefully inserting your fingers between skin and flesh. Push the butter mixture under the skin, easing it over the whole bird. Try not to puncture the skin. Place the lemon half, onion half, garlic and herb sprigs in the turkey's cavity.

3 For the stuffing, heat the olive oil in a frying pan over a medium heat. Add the bacon and cook for 2 minutes. Next add the onions and celery and cook for a further 3 minutes, stirring the pan. Take off the heat and set to one side.

4 Make the parsley and thyme stuffing following the packet instructions and add the melted butter and lemon rind to it. Then add the bacon mixture to the bowl and mix well.

5 Fill the neck cavity with the stuffing. Preheat the oven to 200°C or 400°F or gas mark 6.

6 Place the remaining three chunked onions, the 12 bay leaves and half the stock in the bottom of a roasting tray, place a rack over this mixture and put the turkey on the rack (if you don't have a rack, just put the turkey on the onions). Brush the turkey with the melted butter and season with salt and pepper. Place in the oven and cook for 2 hours.

7 After 1 hour, cover the breast and end of the drumsticks with foil if they look too brown. Pour extra stock into the roasting tray from time to time.

8 Reduce the oven temperature to 180°C or 350°F or gas mark 4 and return the turkey to the oven on another ovenproof dish for 25 minutes, while you make the gravy.

9 Remove the rack from the roasting tray and place the tray over a medium heat on the stove. Remove as much fat from the juices in the pan as possible (but don't worry if a little remains). Add the red wine and redcurrant jelly to the pan and, with a wooden spoon, scrape the bottom of the pan to loosen any bits that have stuck. Simmer gently until the jelly melts.

10 Mix the cornflour with a little water to pouring consistency and stir into the sauce, until it thickens slightly. Season to taste. Strain the sauce into a jug and keep warm.

11 Remove the turkey from the oven and allow to stand for 15 minutes. Remove the foil and serve with the gravy and normal accompaniments.

After today it's cold turkey on booze, and cold turkey sandwiches

CHRISTMAS CLUB SANDWICH

Serves 4
12 slices country bread
unsalted butter
turkey stuffing & cranberry sauce
brown and white turkey meat
turkey gravy
baked ham, sliced
tomatoes, sliced
mayonnaise
salt and freshly ground black pepper

1 Spread the bread with butter (one side only). Lay four slices on a work surface, butter-side up, and top with a layer of stuffing, then a layer of cranberry sauce followed by the turkey meat.

2 Spread the turkey with cold gravy, top with another slice of bread, then layers of ham, tomato and mayonnaise. Season, and top with the final slice of bread, butter-side down. Serve with a glass of mulled wine.

2

Beef

Buying & cooking beef

After a ruinous decade of BSE and foot-and-mouth disease, the UK beef industry is slowly finding its feet again, but it may take another ten years to convince consumers that Britain is producing beef that knocks the spots off the rest of the world. Intensive farming has been the scourge of our food industry, but it's here to stay unless the public makes more noises about quality rather than cost.

It's simple: you get what you pay for. When I opened my Notting Grill restaurant in London, I made a decision to buy only the best. I pay a little more, but I know I'm giving my customers some of the best beef in the UK. I stand by our slogan: 'well-bred, well-fed, well-hung!' *I'm* not going to compromise, nor should *you*.

If you're worried about the price of the best cuts – fillet, sirloin, rib and rump – then try the forequarter of the animal: the bit that provides all the stewing and braising cuts. If we returned to the great stews of yesteryear and good, slow cooking, then we would give farmers a use for cheaper cuts. This, in turn, would mean that prime cuts could come down in price.

Try some of the traditional cattle breeds: Aberdeen Angus (the pure breed, not the fifty percent cross), Longhorn, Dexter, Welsh Black, Ruby Red, Hereford, etc. If we don't support our own breeds, they will disappear, leaving only Continental crosses. Also, try to find a butcher who understands the welfare and the feeding of cattle.

Now, what do I look for when buying beef? 'Lean' has been the message for years, yet it's fat that gives beef its flavour. Look for yellowing fat, and if buying grilling or roasting cuts, look for marbling: the small rivulets of fat that run through the meat. Supermarkets often sell topside joints for roasting – a big mistake. This cut is best braised, as it is devoid of fat and can be very tough. Look for beef that has a darker, reddish-brown flesh which indicates age, rather than the bright-red, spanking-new-looking meat which tells you it's from a recent kill.

Grilling

I don't recommend this method, as home grills aren't hot enough to seal the meat. If you have a barbecue or an indoor chargrill, that's fine; otherwise, use a griddle or ridged pan to simulate grilling. Cuts for grilling include sirloin, rump, T-bone, fillet and *onglet*: a French cut best represented by the English skirt cut, a piece found on the inside of the ribs. If I'm grilling or frying a steak, I like it at least two inches thick. Cook one steak of 500g (1 lb 4 oz) for two and slice it on the diagonal.

Frying

Follow similar rules to grilling, using a very hot pan to seal the meat before reducing the temperature. Don't salt the meat until just prior to or during cooking, as it will draw out the blood and toughen the meat.

Boiling

I have a particular soft spot for that classic dish, Boiled Beef and Carrots. Use silverside or brisket, salted if you want a red hue to the meat. Cook very slowly in water or stock (up to four hours, or until the meat is tender) with a bouquet of root vegetables, a few herbs and a pig's trotter for extra richness.

Roasting

This demands a quality cut of meat. I would recommend rib of beef on the bone, or rolled rib off the bone. You can also roast fillet and sirloin, but avoid those lean favourites silverside, topside and brisket. I prefer to seal my joint in a hot pan before putting it into a hot oven.

Season with salt, pepper and a fine film of Dijon mustard if desired. Place the meat on a rack above a pan of dripping, roast potatoes or Yorkshire pudding, allowing the meat to drip delicious juices onto whatever you cook below. If you prefer to cook the beef in a roasting pan, place it on a layer of sliced carrots, onions and potatoes. This will keep the joint off the surface of the hot pan, preventing a thick crust from forming. Baste the roast regularly during cooking.

I prefer to roast for a shorter time in a hotter oven, 220°C (425°F or gas mark 7). Always allow the meat to rest for ten to fifteen minutes before carving. Carved straight from the oven, all the juices will end up in your carving dish and you won't find an even colour throughout the meat.

Braising and pot-roasting

These are two of the most delicious forms of cooking. For both methods, it is possible to use cheaper cuts of beef, such as topside or silverside, ideally larded with pork fat. Again, for both methods, one piece of meat is used, normally dusted in seasoned flour then browned in dripping or oil.

For braising, the meat sits on a bed of root vegetables with enough wine or stock to come halfway up the meat. Long, slow cooking makes for tender meat packed full of flavour; cook for two to five hours at 150°C (300°F or gas mark 2), depending on the size of the joint. Pot-roasting is similar, except cut back on the liquor and increase the butter.

Stewing

Stewing is very similar to braising, except that the meat is cut into bite-size pieces. This allows you to buy even cheaper cuts from the shin, leg of beef, chuck, blade, neck and skirt. Some of the most delicious dishes fall into this category: boeuf bourguignon, goulash, estouffades and carbonnades.

In time, if more people are lured back to this sort of cooking, bargains and delicious flavours will be enjoyed all round.

Stir-frying

As Britain becomes a culinary magpie, so this form of cookery becomes more and more popular. Stir-frying is ideally suited to the more tender cuts of meat such as sirloin, rump or the tail end of fillet.

STEAK AU POIVRE

Serves 2
450g or 1 lb rump steak, 4cm (1½ inches) thick
3 tsp cracked black peppercorns
1 tbsp olive oil
2 tbsp brandy
1 tsp French mustard
1 tsp Worcestershire sauce
4 tbsp beef stock
2 tbsp red wine
1 tbsp green peppercorns in brine, drained
4 tbsp double cream
25g or 1 oz unsalted butter
salt to taste

1 Preheat the oven to 190°C or 375°F or gas mark 5. Press the cracked pepper into both sides of the steak. Heat a heavy-based iron frying pan over a high heat, add the oil and, when it is slightly smoking, add the steak. Cook for 2 minutes on each side.

2 Place in the oven and cook for a further 8 minutes for a rare steak, longer if desired. Remove from the oven and set the meat aside to rest. Keep it warm.

3 Over a medium heat, add the brandy to the frying pan, scrape up all the meat juices, then add the mustard, Worcestershire sauce, beef stock and red wine. Whisk to combine, and cook until the sauce has reduced by a third. Pour into the sauce any juices that have seeped from the beef. Add the green peppercorns, cream and butter and cook for a further 2 minutes. Season to taste with salt.

4 Slice the steak on the diagonal and add to the sauce. Stir to combine the meat juices with the pepper sauce and warm the meat through (but do not re-boil). Serve with chips or new potatoes and a watercress salad.

ROAST RIB OF BEEF
IN A HERB CRUST

Serves 8-10
1 x 4-rib piece Angus beef on the bone
  (trimmed weight approximately
  4kg or 10 lb), chined
2 tbsp black peppercorns
2 bay leaves, dried
1 tsp dried thyme
55g or 2 oz unsalted butter, softened
1 tbsp Dijon mustard
2 tbsp plain flour
1 tsp ground white pepper
1 tsp Maldon sea salt
500g or 1 lb 2 oz banana shallots, peeled
2 heads garlic, separated into unpeeled cloves
500g or 1 lb 2 oz carrots, peeled,
  quartered lengthways
2 sprigs thyme
600ml or 20 fl oz beef consommé

For the gravy
375ml or a half-bottle dry red wine
1 tsp anchovy essence, (optional)
1 tbsp redcurrant jelly
1 tsp mushroom ketchup
1 tsp Worcestershire sauce
1 tbsp cornflour (optional)

The plat du jour
is herb crust with
a hint of beef

METHOD

1 Stand the beef at room temperature for half an hour to an hour. Meanwhile, in a spice mill or coffee grinder, grind together the peppercorns, bay leaves and thyme to a fine powder.

2 In a separate bowl, combine the butter, mustard, flour, white pepper and salt. Beat thoroughly, then fold in the herb powder. Smear the beef all over with this butter mix.

3 In an oven preheated to 240°C (475°F, gas mark 9), cook the beef, rib-side down, for 30 minutes. Reduce the heat to 180°C (350°F, gas mark 4) for another 1½ hours, or until a meat thermometer inserted registers 55-60°C (130-140°F) for rare or 80°C (175°F) for well-done.

4 Fifty minutes before the meat is done, add the shallots, garlic, carrots and thyme; toss in the fat. Add a small amount of consommé, then return to the oven. Continue to add consommé every 10 minutes. This is your gravy base.

5 Remove the meat, shallots, garlic and carrots to a carving dish to keep warm. Allow them to rest for 20 minutes while you make the gravy.

6 Pour the cooking fats and juices into a bowl to settle. Remove the fats from the top and reserve in your dripping pot. Place the roasting tray on the hob over a medium heat. Add the red wine and de-glaze the pan, scraping up any bits that have stuck to the bottom. Mash the garlic reserved from earlier.

7 Add the anchovy essence (if using), the redcurrant jelly, the mushroom ketchup, Worcestershire sauce and meat juices and stir to combine. Mix the cornflour to a paste with a little water; fold into the boiling gravy. Strain and pour into a gravy boat. Serve the gravy with the roast, shallots and carrots and any other desired vegetables – together with Yorkshire puddings, of course.

FILLET OF BEEF STROGANOFF

Serves 2
4 tbsp flour
2 tbsp paprika
1 tsp salt
280g or 10 oz beef fillet, cut into 6cm x 1cm
*   (2½ inch x ½-inch) strips*
1 tbsp olive oil
25g or 1 oz unsalted butter
1 shallot, peeled and finely chopped
115g or 4 oz button mushrooms, quartered
2 tbsp brandy
1 tsp French mustard
1 tsp Worcestershire sauce
4 tbsp beef stock
2 tbsp red wine
4 tbsp sour cream
juice of ½ lemon
salt to taste

1 Combine the flour, paprika and salt. Coat
the beef in seasoned flour. Heat a heavy-based

frying pan over a high heat, add the oil and, when hot, the strips of beef. Cook until brown but still rare, about 3 minutes. Remove the beef from the pan and set aside to keep warm.

2 Over a medium heat, add the butter, shallots and mushrooms to the skillet and cook for 5 minutes. Add the brandy; scrape up the meat juices, then add the mustard, Worcestershire sauce, beef stock and red wine. Whisk and cook until the sauce has reduced by a third.

3 Pour into the sauce any juices that have seeped from the beef. Add the sour cream and lemon juice; cook for a further 2 minutes. Season to taste with salt. Return the meat to the pan to warm, about 2 minutes, but do not boil.

4 Serve immediately with buttered rice and a dollop of sour cream, sprinkled with paprika.

Steak Diane

For a modern touch with this recipe, you can use half butter and half oil. If using a non-stick pan, reduce by half the total amount of fat in the recipe.

Serves 4
85g or 3 oz butter
2 shallots, finely chopped
2 tbsp chopped parsley
4 minute steaks, about 175g or 6 oz each
salt and freshly ground black pepper
1–2 tsp Worcestershire sauce
2 tbsp brandy

1 Heat the butter in a large frying pan. Fry the seasoned steaks for 1½ minutes each side. Remove and keep warm.

2 Add the shallots and half the parsley and cook for 4 to 6 minutes, or until the shallots are nearly tender.

3 Add the Worcestershire sauce. Heat for a few seconds. Pour in the brandy, stir well to mix it with the other ingredients, then ignite.

4 Top with the remaining parsley and serve. In restaurants, chipped potatoes and peas are the usual accompaniments.

STEAK TARTARE WITH
BUTTER-FRIED OYSTERS

Serves 2

*275g or 9½ oz beef fillet or sirloin, trimmed
of fat and finely chopped*

1 tbsp finely chopped shallot

1 tbsp finely chopped flat-leaf parsley

2 tsp Dijon mustard

2 tsp chopped gherkin

1 tsp chopped capers

2 chopped anchovies

1 tsp finely diced chilli (or Tabasco sauce)

1 tsp Worcestershire sauce

1 raw egg yolk

salt and freshly ground black pepper

55g or 2 oz butter

12 oysters

1 Combine the first 11 ingredients in a mixing bowl, and blend with a fork until just mixed. Form into two 'burgers' and refrigerate until ready to eat.

2 Heat some of the butter in a frying pan until foaming, fry the oysters and add them six at a time. Cook over a fierce heat, until the edges curl, turning once, about 1 minute.

3 Remove, then repeat with the second six, adding extra butter as necessary. Season to taste.

4 Heat the oyster base shells in the oven. Place one oyster in each shell and arrange around the two steak tartares. Serve with thin chips.

Spaghetti Bolognaise

Serves 6
150ml or 5 fl oz good olive oil
55g or 2 oz streaky bacon, diced
1 onion, finely diced
1 celery stick, finely diced
1 carrot, finely diced
2 garlic cloves, crushed
1 tsp soft thyme leaves
1 bay leaf
1 tsp dried oregano
1 x 400g or 14 oz can chopped tomatoes
1 tbsp tomato purée
1½ tsp anchovy essence
1 tbsp Worcestershire sauce
salt and freshly ground black pepper
900g or 2 lb minced beef (coarsely ground)
115g or 4 oz fresh chicken livers, finely chopped
1 bottle dry red wine
1 litre (35 fl oz) fresh chicken, lamb, or beef stock
450g or 1 lb dried spaghetti
freshly grated Parmesan cheese, to garnish

1 Heat a large, heavy-based saucepan. Add 2 tablespoons of the oil and tip in the bacon. Cook for a couple of minutes until crispy, then add the onion, celery, carrot, garlic, thyme, bay leaf and oregano and cook over a medium heat until the vegetables have softened and taken on a little colour, stirring occasionally.

2 Add the canned tomatoes, tomato purée, anchovy essence and Worcestershire sauce. Stir and season to taste.

3 Meanwhile, heat a large frying pan. Add a little oil and fry the minced beef in small batches until browned. Break up any lumps with the back of a wooden spoon. Repeat the process until all of the meat is browned.

4 Drain off any fat and stir the meat into the tomato mixture.

5 Wipe out the pan with some kitchen paper and add a little more oil, then fry the chicken livers until sizzling and lightly browned.

6 Tip the liver into the minced-beef mixture, then de-glaze the frying pan with some of the red wine, scraping any sediment from the bottom with a wooden spoon. Pour this wine, along with the rest of the wine and the stock, into the minced-beef mixture, stirring to combine.

7 Bring to a boil, then reduce the heat. Simmer very gently, stirring occasionally, for about 2 hours (up to 4 is fine), or until the beef is completely tender and the liquid has been reduced. Season to taste. Top up with a little water if necessary. If time allows, leave to cool, then chill until the fat solidifies on the top. Carefully remove it and discard.

8 Gently reheat the bolognaise sauce. Bring a large pan of water to a rolling boil. Add a good pinch of salt and a dash of the olive oil. Swirl in the spaghetti, stir once and cook for eight to 12 minutes, or until *al dente*. Drain and divide among serving bowls.

9 Spoon over the meat sauce, sprinkle with the Parmesan and serve at once.

THAI BEEF SALAD

Serves 4
1 tbsp soy sauce
1 dessertspoon runny honey
juice of 2 limes
1 tsp sesame oil
1 tbsp sweet chilli sauce
2 garlic cloves, mashed with a little salt
1 tsp freshly grated ginger
450g or 1 lb leftover rare beef from your
  Sunday roast, thinly sliced and cut
  into julienne strips
½ cucumber peeled, deseeded,
  cut into 2.5cm (1-inch) batons
½ red onion, finely sliced
1 punnet cherry tomatoes, halved
1 tbsp fresh mint leaves, roughly chopped
1 tbsp fresh coriander leaves, roughly chopped
2 baby gem lettuces, washed, leaves separated
1 tbsp roasted peanuts, roughly chopped

1 Combine the first seven ingredients to make the dressing.

2 Combine the remaining ingredients (except for the lettuce and peanuts) with the dressing. Place onto the baby gem lettuce leaves and garnish with a sprinkling of chopped roasted peanuts, if desired.

3 Serve immediately with some lime wedges for a refreshing summer salad.

THE PERFECT STEAK SANDWICH
WITH WARM TOMATO SALSA

Serves 2
2 tbsp balsamic vinegar
1 garlic clove, finely chopped
1 small dried chilli, crushed
1 tsp freshly chopped oregano
2 x 115g–150g or 4 oz–5 oz sirloin steaks,
    1 cm or ½ inch thick

For the warm tomato salsa
2 tbsp olive oil
1 red onion, finely sliced
1 garlic clove, chopped
1 small dried chilli
350g or 12 oz baby plum tomatoes
1 tbsp balsamic vinegar
1 tbsp fresh oregano, finely chopped

For the salad
2 large handfuls wild rocket
55g or 2 oz Roquefort cheese
salt and freshly ground pepper

4 thick slices of sourdough bread
55g or 2 oz unsalted butter, softened

1 Mix the balsamic vinegar, garlic, chilli, oregano in a shallow dish. Add the steaks and marinade for 15 to 30 minutes.

2 Fifteen minutes before cooking, make the salsa. Heat the oil gently in a frying pan. Add the onion, garlic and chilli; cook gently for 5 to 10 minutes until the onion is soft and golden.

3 Add the tomatoes and cook for 3 to 4 minutes until the tomatoes begin to soften.

Stir in the balsamic vinegar and oregano and cook for another minute. Season.

4 Meanwhile, butter one side of each piece of bread and season. Toast the bread on the buttered side for 1 to 2 minutes and reserve. Place the rocket in a bowl and roughly crumble in the Roquefort.

5 Remove the steaks from the marinade and season with salt and pepper. Sear on a barbecue or grill for 1 minute each side (longer depending upon taste).

6 To assemble the sandwiches, divide the rocket and Roquefort salad between two pieces of the toasted bread and top each with a steak. Spoon over the warm tomato salsa and top each with a piece of toasted bread. Cut each sandwich in half on the diagonal and serve with hot potato wedges.

Beef bourguignon

Serves 6

*1.5kg or 3 lb 5 oz blade or chuck beef steak,
    cut into 5cm or 2-inch cubes*
1 bottle of burgundy wine
plain flour, for coating
salt and freshly ground black pepper
2 tbsp olive oil
200g or 7 oz streaky bacon
12 small onions or 24 shallots, peeled
3 cloves garlic, finely chopped
1 tsp tomato purée
1 tsp anchovy essence or Worcestershire sauce
2-3 stalks parsley
1 sprig thyme
1 bay leaf
18 button mushrooms
300ml or 10 fl oz well-flavoured meat stock
chopped parsley, to serve

METHOD

1 Marinade the beef in the red wine overnight. Drain thoroughly, and dry on kitchen paper.

2 Season the flour and then sprinkle it over the diced beef to cover thoroughly. Shake to remove excess flour.

3 Heat the olive oil in a large frying pan and add some salt and freshly ground black pepper. Add the beef and fry gently for a few minutes until just browned. As each piece of beef becomes browned, remove it from the pan and reserve to one side.

4 Pour out most of the fat from the frying pan and add the bacon, onions or shallots and garlic, and cook gently for 3 to 4 minutes. Add the red wine from the marinade and bring to the boil.

5 Return the meat to the pan, add the tomato purée and anchovy essence or Worcestershire sauce. Mix well and transfer everything to a large casserole dish.

6 Tie the parsley stalks, thyme and bay leaf into a bundle and add to the casserole dish with the mushrooms. Pour in the stock and cook in a preheated oven on 180°C or 350°F or gas mark 4 for a minimum of three hours, but the longer the cooking time, the more tender the meat. To cook it for up to 8 hours: reduce the heat to 140°C (275°F, gas mark 1).

7 To thicken the sauce before serving, remove the beef and pour the liquid into a large saucepan. Bring to the boil and reduce until the sauce thickens. Return the beef to the saucepan to heat through, and serve garnished with chopped parsley and a bowl of hot, buttered new potatoes.

ONION MARMALADE & GORGONZOLA STEAKS

Serves 2
1 tbsp olive oil
salt and freshly ground black pepper
450g or 1 lb rump steak, 4cm (1½ inches) thick
125g or 4½ oz AWT's Onion Marmalade
* (or see recipe opposite)*
85g or 3 oz Gorgonzola cheese, crumbled

1 Pour the olive oil and seasoning onto a plate and coat both sides of the steak. Heat a ridged, cast-iron frying pan over a high heat. Cook the steak for 3 to 6 minutes each side, depending on personal preference.

2 Spoon the onion marmalade on top of the steak while still in the pan. Add the cheese.

3 Put the steaks under a hot grill until the cheese is melted. Serve with new potatoes and a mixed leaf salad.

For the onion marmalade
4 tbsp olive oil
1.5kg or 3 lb 5 oz onions, very thinly sliced
1 tsp rock salt
1 bay leaf
1 tsp soft thyme leaves
1-2 tsp freshly ground black pepper
115g or 4 oz golden caster sugar
2 tbsp each dry sherry & aged red-wine vinegar
375ml or 13 fl oz red wine
1 tbsp runny honey
115g or 4 oz pitted prunes, chopped (optional)

1 Heat the oil in a large, heavy-based pan. Add the onions, salt, bay leaf, thyme and pepper; stir until well-mixed. Reduce the heat, cover and cook for 35 minutes, stirring occasionally, until the onions are softened but not coloured.

2 Stir in the sugar, sherry, vinegar, wine, honey and prunes. Reduce the heat and cook gently, uncovered, for about 1½ or 2 hours, until very dark, stirring every 5 minutes for the last half-hour. Cool, and pack into sterilized glass jars.

SPICY MEATBALLS AND BUTTERNUT SQUASH CASSEROLE

A delicious supper dish that is easy to make – one-pot dining at its best.

Serves 4
For the meatballs
450g or 1 lb minced beef
1 onion, roughly chopped
1 garlic clove, chopped
2 tsp ground cumin
1 tsp ground coriander
a pinch of cayenne pepper
2 tbsp coriander leaves
plain flour, for coating
4 tbsp olive oil
salt and freshly ground black pepper

For the squash casserole
2 tbsp olive oil
1 onion, roughly chopped
2 garlic cloves, finely chopped
1 red pepper, deseeded and roughly chopped
1 chilli, deseeded and finely diced
1 tsp thyme leaves, finely chopped
1 small butternut squash, peeled, deseeded
*   and cut into 1cm or ½-inch cubes*
salt and freshly ground black pepper
1 tbsp mint, chopped

METHOD

1 Blend the minced meat, onion, garlic, ground cumin, ground coriander, cayenne and coriander leaves in a food processor until smooth.

2 Using your hands, take a small handful of the mixture and roll it into a ball. Place the meatballs on a lightly floured tray. Repeat this process until you have used up all the mixture. Refrigerate until ready to cook.

3 Roll the meatballs in the plain flour until they are well-coated. Shallow-fry them in the olive oil until golden, remembering to turn during cooking. Drain on paper towels, and set aside.

4 Meanwhile, make the squash casserole. In a deep frying pan, heat the olive oil. Add the onions, garlic, red peppers, chilli and thyme and cook on a medim heat, until the onions have started to soften but are not coloured.

5 Add the butternut squash and cook, stirring frequently, until the squash is tender – about 15 minutes.

6 Finally, add the meatballs and cook for a further 2 to 3 minutes. Season with salt and freshly ground black pepper to taste, and fold in the chopped mint.

7 Serve with warm pitta bread, a little salad and a dollop of Greek yoghurt.

Peach-bourboned meatballs

Makes 4 starters or 30 meatball canapés
1.3kg or 3 lb minced beef
300ml or 10 fl oz milk
1 free-range egg, beaten
55g or 2 oz fresh white breadcrumbs
1 shallot, finely chopped
1½ tbsp Worcestershire sauce
2 tsp salt
2 garlic cloves, finely chopped
½ tsp each ground nutmeg & ground ginger
½ tsp freshly ground black pepper
2 tbsp chopped parsley
1 tsp Tabasco sauce
55g or 2 oz unsalted butter

For the peach Bourbon sauce
1 jar peach jam
200g or 7 oz soft brown sugar
150ml or 5 fl oz Bourbon
150ml or 5 fl oz orange marmalade
¼ tsp each nutmeg & ground ginger
1½ tbsp cornflour & 1 tbsp water

1 Blend the first 12 ingredients together in a bowl and shape the mixture into 2.5cm (1-inch) balls. Pan-fry the meatballs in the butter until brown all over. Remove and keep warm.

2 Combine the ingredients for the Bourbon peach sauce; add to the meat drippings in the pan. Bring to a simmer; cook for 10 minutes.

3 Add the meatballs to this sauce and simmer for 30 minutes. Remove the meatballs and, if the sauce is not thick enough, blend the cornflour with the water and add, stirring constantly, cooking until thick.

4 Serve the sauce and meatballs separately with cocktail sticks.

Kofta pitta bread

Serves 6
1kg or 2 lb 4 oz lean minced beef
1 onion, peeled and grated
6 tbsp chopped flat-leaf parsley, chopped
2 tbsp chopped mint
2 tsp ground cumin
1 tsp salt
1 tsp freshly ground black pepper
olive oil, for frying

For the pitta sandwich
6 pitta breads
1 cucumber, peeled, deseeded, cut in small dice
6 plum tomatoes, deseeded, cut in small dice

For the sauce
300ml or 10 fl oz thick Greek yoghurt
8 dried apricots, finely diced
2 garlic cloves, peeled and finely chopped
1 tbsp chopped mint
salt and cayenne pepper

1 In a food processor, blend together the minced meat, onion, parsley, mint, cumin, salt and pepper until smooth. Shape the meat into 12 oval flat patties or, if serving with rice, into 24 meatballs.

2 Steam the pitta bread in foil over boiling water and cut a slash in the side of each to create a pocket. For the sauce, combine all the ingredients and season to taste.

3 Pan-fry the patties in hot olive oil in a frying pan for 3 to 4 minutes each side.

4 Spoon 2 tablespoons each of tomato and cucumber into each pitta, then slip in two koftas. Top with a spoonful of the yoghurt sauce. Alternatively, cut the pitta in two horizontally to create two pockets and follow the same procedure, using one kofta instead of two.

STEAK & KIDNEY PUDDING

Serves 6-8
750g or 1 lb 10 oz chuck or blade beef steak,
  cut into 2.5cm or 1-inch cubes
225g or 8 oz ox kidney, cut into 2.5 cm
  or 1-inch cubes
1 small onion, finely chopped
large pinch celery salt
1 tsp fresh thyme leaves
salt and freshly ground black pepper
2 tbsp plain flour
up to 150ml or 5 fl oz fresh beef stock

For the suet pastry
400g or 14oz self-raising flour (extra for dusting)
½ tsp of salt
200g or 7 oz beef or vegetarian suet
freshly ground black pepper
300ml or 10 fl oz cold water
unsalted butter, for greasing

mashed potatoes and buttered peas, to serve

1 Place the steak and kidney into a large bowl. Stir in the onion, celery salt, thyme and seasoning. Mix together lightly and set to one side, or cover with clingfilm and chill for up to 24 hours to allow the flavours to combine.

2 To make the suet pastry, sieve the flour and salt into a large bowl. Add the suet and season with pepper. Lightly mix and then add the cold water, a little at a time, cutting through the dough with a round-bladed knife as if you were making scones. Using your hands, mix to form a soft dough.

3 Roll out the pastry on a lightly floured work surface into a round approximately .5 to 1cm (¼ to ½ inches) thick. Cut one-quarter of the pastry to within 2.5cm (1 inch) of the centre; set aside for the lid. Use the remaining pastry to line a well-buttered 1.7 litre or 3-pint pudding basin, leaving at least 2.5cm (1 inch) of pastry hanging over the edge.

4 Add the flour to the steak and kidney mixture and stir gently to combine. Place the batches of meat mixture into a sieve (with a glass bowl underneath) and shake to remove any excess flour.

5 Spoon the lightly coated meat mixture into the lined pudding basin, being careful not to press it down, then pour in enough of the beef stock to come to nearly two-thirds to the top, not covering the meat completely.

6 Roll out the remaining pastry circle 2.5cm (1 inch) larger than the top of the basin. Dampen the edges of the pastry lining the basin, place the lid over the filling and press the two edges together to seal; trim off any excess. Make two small slits in the top.

7 Cover the pudding with a double piece of buttered foil, pleated in the centre to allow for expansion while cooking. Secure it with a piece of string, making a handle so that you can easily lift it out of the hot steamer.

8 Place the pudding on an upturned plate in a large pan filled two-thirds up the side of the basin with hot water. Steam for 5 hours, topping up with boiling water occasionally so as not to allow the pan to boil dry.

9 Remove the pudding basin from the pan. Cut the string from the basin and remove the foil. Wrap the pudding basin in a folded clean napkin to serve.

3
Pork

Pork   porker   porkest

Buying & cooking pork

Pork is probably the meat in which I have the most interest, as I breed my own Middle White pigs and am patron of the Middle White Breeders Club. What a difference a breed makes! Some of the white stuff sold under the guise of pork is nothing short of scandalous; fat-free, dry and leathery, is it no wonder that fewer people are eating pork.

It's tender as veal, but unlike veal, it is a meat with real flavour and the best crackling in the world. But that's my bias; you may prefer one of the other rare traditional breeds: Gloucester Old Spot, Large White, Tamworth, Saddleback, etc. Preserving these breeds is down to us. We should at least be encouraging farmers to cross the common hybrid with a rare breed. Intensive farming is here to stay, but it would help if decent breeds were used.

If you can, avoid intensively reared pigs; their living and feeding conditions make for horrendous reading. Opt for free-range, runabout pigs that will have a magical flavour.

Which parts to eat

From head to tail, here are the edible parts of a pig. The HEAD yields brains, tongue, throat, jowl, ear, lips and snout: all great for salting and using in head cheese or brawn. HOCKS, TROTTERS, SHANKS, TAILS and EARS lend themselves to being poached, spread with mustard and breadcrumbs and grilled until crisp.

Inside the pig lie the HEART, LIVER and KIDNEYS, the BLADDER, the STOMACH (or TRIPE) and INTESTINES. Next, we have the SHOULDER, which provides roasting and braising joints, meat for stewing and mincing and sausages. The LOIN is the most expensive cut, providing chops, loin roast, and fillet, and in its salted form, back bacon. The BELLY provides belly chops, streaky bacon, spare ribs and meat for terrines. Finally, the LEG yields the best roasting joints, whole hams and cubes of pork for kebabs.

The colour of pork varies from pale-pink to pale-red, according to the pig's age and the cut of meat. Look for meat that has very white fat and flesh that appears dry. You probably won't be able to find out, but where possible buy pork from sow meat rather than boar. Trim away some of the fat from the pork before cooking. Use the fat to make a dripping by rendering, or mince it and freeze it, adding it to stews, stuffings or terrines.

To roast pork

Marinate, stuff it or leave the joint as it is. Brown the meat all over before roasting it at 200°C or 400°F or gas mark 6 for 20 minutes, then reduce the heat for the remainder of the cooking time. Allow 25 to 30 minutes per 500g (1 lb 2 oz). If you like crackling, score the rind in thin strips, pour boiling water over the rind three times, then baste with cider vinegar. Leave uncovered in the fridge overnight. The next day, rub the rind with coarse salt and olive oil, and roast in the normal way.

To grill pork

Brush each side with oil or melted butter. Season just before cooking. A normal chop should take five to seven minutes per side. If you are cooking pork chops with the rind, score it to prevent the chop from curling.

To stir-fry

Fry in hot oil for one minute, remove meat, add the remaining stir-fry ingredients then fold back the meat to warm through.

To braise or stew

Braising uses large cuts of meat and stews use diced meat. Both require the meat to be browned then cooked very slowly with vegetables, liquid and aromatics until it is very tender.

ROAST PORK, GREAT CRACKLING AND APPLE SAUCE

Serves 6
2kg or 4 lb 8 oz leg of pork (½ leg),
with the rind scored
4 tbsp cider vinegar
8 sage leaves
3 tbsp pork dripping or butter
2 tbsp Maldon sea salt
1 tbsp crushed black peppercorns
8 bay leaves
6 sage leaves
8 unpeeled garlic cloves
1 glass dry white wine
600ml or 20 fl oz chicken stock
2 Bramley apples, peeled, cored and cubed
juice of ½ lemon
1 tbsp caster sugar

1 The night before, pour boiling water over the pork rind three times at 1-minute intervals. This Oriental method helps tighten

the rind and yields better crackling. Baste the raw joint with cider vinegar, rubbing it all over to ensure the vinegar gets into the rind. Place on a plate in the fridge, uncovered, overnight.

2 Preheat the oven to 200°C or 400°F or gas mark 6. Make eight cuts in the pork and insert the eight sage leaves into the cuts. Spread the pork with the dripping or butter, then the salt and pepper.

3 Place in a roasting tray with the bay leaves, sage and garlic. Pour in the wine and 150ml (5 fl oz) of the chicken stock and place in the oven. Roast for half an hour, then reduce the oven temperature to 180°C or 350°F or gas mark 4. Roast for a further 1½ hours.

4 Remove the pork from the roasting pan. Rest it for fifteen minutes in a warm place.

5 Put the roasting tray over a medium heat. Scrape any crusted bits from the bottom of the tray and add the remaining chicken stock. Boil and reduce until you are left with 300ml (10 fl oz) of liquid. Strain the liquid into a gravy boat and skim off any fat. Add any juices that have collected under the resting joint. Season to taste.

6 Meanwhile, cook the apples over a medium heat with 2 tbsp water, the lemon juice and the sugar until soft and broken down. Serve warm or cold.

7 Carve off the crackling in one piece and cut into portions. Serve the pork with the apple sauce, gravy, roast potatoes and a selection of vegetables.

CRISPY BACON HASH

Serves 2
4 slices streaky bacon, diced
1 tbsp olive oil
25g or 1 oz unsalted butter
1 onion, roughly chopped
2 cooked potatoes, peeled and diced
1 chilli, finely diced
1 garlic clove, finely chopped
1 tsp soft thyme leaves
1 tbsp chopped parsley

1 In a non-stick pan, fry the bacon until crispy; remove and set aside.

2 Add the oil and butter and cook the onion until soft and slightly caramelized. Add the potato, chilli, garlic and bacon, and cook until the potato is golden, stirring regularly.

3 Season to taste and add the herbs. Serve with poached eggs.

POACHED PORK SHOULDER

Serves 4

1 large onion, thinly sliced
1 carrot, sliced
1 boneless pork shoulder joint,
*   1.5 kg or 3 lb 5 oz*
1 bottle dry white wine
1 litre or 35 fl oz chicken stock
1 tsp sea salt
2 tsp chopped ginger
1 tsp black peppercorns
4 dried chillies
1 clove
1 tbsp liquid honey
1 star anise
1 head garlic, cut in half horizontally
2 tsp coriander seed
1 tsp cumin seed
2 bay leaves
2 stalks celery, sliced
2 tbsp chopped coriander leaves

1 Place the onion and carrots in a medium-sized saucepan. Put the pork on top of this vegetable bed. Add the remaining ingredients.

2 Bring to the boil over a medium heat, then reduce the heat, cover and simmer for 1 hour and 15 minutes, skimming from time to time. Halfway through cooking, turn the pork shoulder over.

3 As the pork cooks, the liquid will reduce, so in the last minutes of cooking, baste the pork every 10 minutes with the stock.

4 Serve hot with potatoes and some good strong mustard. If serving cold, allow the meat to cool in the liquor. After removing the meat, strain the stock and remove any fat. The stock can be frozen for use in soups and stews.

TOAD IN THE HOLE

Serves 4
8 pork sausages, Duchy Original or Musk's
2 tbsp Dijon mustard
4 tbsp of beef dripping
2 onions, finely sliced

For the batter
115g or 4 oz plain flour
large pinch of salt
4 eggs
300ml or 10 fl oz milk
2 tbsp of fresh thyme leaves
freshly ground black pepper

1 To make the batter, sift the flour and salt into a large bowl. Make a well in the centre and break in the eggs. Gradually beat the eggs into the flour using a wooden spoon and slowly add the milk until the batter coats the back of the spoon. Stir in the thyme, season with black pepper, cover and let stand for 30 minutes.

2 Preheat the oven to 220°C or 425°F or gas mark 7. Cook the sausages in a large frying pan over a medium heat until golden brown all over. Remove from the pan, brush with the mustard and set aside. Add a little dripping to the pan and fry the onions until golden, about 10 minutes.

3 Put the dripping into a roasting dish and place in the oven for 5 minutes, or until the dripping is hot and almost smoking.

4 Add the sausages and onions to the hot roasting tin; pour in the batter. Immediately return the tin to the oven and bake for 35 to 40 minutes, until well-risen and golden. If the batter is becoming too brown, reduce the heat to 190°C or 375°F or gas mark 5.

5 Serve with gravy and a green vegetable.

ASIAN PORK MEATBALLS

Serves 4-6
55g or 2 oz caster sugar
3 tbsp Thai fish sauce (nam pla)
450g or 1 lb minced pork
4 spring onions, finely chopped
1 tsp garlic, minced
2 tsp lemon grass, finely chopped
1 tsp cornflour
1 tbsp mint, finely chopped
2 tbsp coriander, finely chopped
half tsp each salt & freshly ground black pepper
olive oil

1 Place the sugar in a non-stick frying pan and heat gently. When it begins to caramelize and turn golden, add the fish sauce.

2 Carefully fold the sugar into the minced pork. Add the spring onions, garlic, lemon grass, cornflour, mint and coriander; mix thoroughly. Season with salt and black pepper.

3 Form the mixture into one-inch meatballs and place onto a tray lined with greaseproof paper. Put in the fridge for 30 minutes before cooking.

4 Brush each meatball lightly with olive oil. Heat a non-stick frying pan with a little oil and pan-fry the meatballs for 12 minutes, turning regularly. Serve with Oriental dipping sauce.

Oriental dipping sauce
1 tsp chopped coriander leaves
3 spring onions, finely sliced
1 tsp grated ginger
1 garlic clove, finely diced
1 chilli, deseeded and finely diced
2 tbsp each fresh lime juice & light soy sauce
1 tsp sesame oil
1 tbsp liquid honey

Simply mix all the ingredients together and set aside until ready to use.

PORK WITH STOUT, PEPPER & BROWN SUGAR

Serves 4
For the marinade
4 tsp freshly ground black peppercorns,
  well-crushed
2 tsp salt
2 tsp dried oregano
1 tsp thyme leaves
4 cloves garlic
2 tbsp soft brown sugar
2 tbsp olive oil
2 tbsp wine vinegar

½ boneless pork shoulder joint,
*   1kg or 2 lb 2 oz*
6 pitted prunes, halved
6 tinned anchovies, cut in half lengthways
85g or 3 oz unsalted butter
1–2 tbsp oil
3 onions, finely sliced
half a tbsp chopped sage
500ml or 18 fl oz Young's Luxury Double-
*   chocolate Stout or a dark Irish stout*
450ml or 16 fl oz chicken stock

METHOD

1 Make the marinade by combining the peppercorns, salt, herbs, garlic and sugar in a food processor, then gradually adding the oil and wine vinegar.

2 Make 12 incisions in the piece of pork. Carefully press half a prune and an anchovy fillet into each slit. Rub with the marinade and leave to marinate in a cool place for at least 3 hours, or ideally overnight.

3 Wipe off the marinade and brown the pork in a casserole dish in half the oil and half the butter, until brown on all sides.

4 Remove the pork and set aside. Add the remaining butter and oil, heat gently and, once foaming, add the onions and sage.

5 Allow the onion to cook over a gentle heat until it caramelizes; this will take about 20

minutes. Preheat the oven to 150°C or 300°F or gas mark 2.

6 After 20 minutes, place the pork back on top of the onion slices in the casserole. Add the marinade, the stout and chicken stock, bring to the boil, and cover the casserole.

7 Cook in the oven for about 4½ hours, until the meat is very tender and able to be cut with a spoon. Remove the meat and keep warm.

8 Pour all the pan juices into a food processor and blend until smooth. If the liquid is too thin, boil vigorously to reduce. Pour over the meat.

9 Serve with roast carrots, roast parsnips and mashed potatoes.

PORK SALTIMBOCCA WITH MOZZARELLA

Serves 4
8 x 85g or 3 oz pork fillet escalopes
8 slices Parma or Serrano ham
8 fresh sage leaves
175g or 6 oz plain flour
115g or 4 oz butter
1 tbsp olive oil
300ml or 10 fl oz dry white wine
8 slices buffalo mozzarella
juice of 1 lemon
salt and freshly ground black pepper
8 finely chopped sage leaves, for the sauce

1 Pound the escalopes to an even thickness of about 5mm (¼ inch). Place a sage leaf on the pork and top with a slice of ham. Dust each slice with flour.

2 In a large frying pan, cook half the pork, ham-side down, over a medium heat in half the butter and oil until browned. Turn over and cook pork-side down for 30 seconds. Remove and set aside to keep warm. Repeat with remaining escalopes.

3 Pour wine into the pan and turn up the heat, allowing the wine to evaporate quickly.

4 Put a slice of mozzarella on top of each escalope and flash under the grill for 2 minutes.

5 While the pork is under the grill, add the remaining butter to the sauce in the pan and stir together. Add the lemon juice, seasoning and chopped sage leaves; stir to combine. To serve, pour the sauce over the pork.

TREACLE-GLAZED
BAKED HAM

Serves 4
1 small joint of boiling bacon
300ml or 10 fl oz cider vinegar
600ml or 20 fl oz dark beer
2 oranges, studded with 2 cloves
2 bay leaves
2 apples, cut in half
2 onions
2 carrots
2 sticks celery
2 sprigs thyme
1 cinnamon stick
a few whole cloves

For the glaze
225g or 8 oz black treacle
55g or 2 oz polenta
1 tbsp dry mustard
1 tbsp black pepper
3 tbsp Bourbon
425ml or 15 fl oz apple juice or cider
150ml or 5 fl oz Madeira or Marsala
225g or 8 oz dried, stoned apricots

METHOD

1 Place the bacon in a large saucepan and add enough water to cover completely. Add all the ingredients except the cloves to the pan and bring to the boil. Simmer gently for 15 minutes per 450g (1 lb).

2 Allow the ham to cool in the cooking liquid. Cut off all the rind, and score the fat in a diamond pattern. Insert a clove in the cross point of each diamond.

3 To make the glaze, in a large bowl, mix together the treacle, polenta, mustard and pepper. Moisten the mixture with the Bourbon. Spread the mixture over the ham.

4 Place the ham in a baking tray and pour the apple juice or cider, Madeira or Marsala around the ham, then add the apricots.

5 Bake in a hot oven (200°C, 400°F or gas mark 6) for about 15 minutes per pound, basting frequently. If the pan starts to burn, add a little water to keep the apricots sticky but not too dark.

6 Serve the sliced ham with the glazed apricots and some lovely buttery mash.

BACON CROISSANT BUTTIE

Makes 8
2 onions, peeled and sliced
1 tsp soft thyme leaves
55g or 2 oz unsalted butter
125g or 4 oz button mushrooms, sliced
salt and freshly ground black pepper
8 slices back bacon, rind removed
8 croissant
Dijon mustard
175g or 6 oz grated Gruyère or
*   Cheddar cheese*

1 Preheat oven to 180°C or 350°F or gas mark 4. Cook the onion and thyme leaves in butter until soft, but not brown, about 8 minutes. Add the mushrooms and cook for 5 minutes. Season to taste with the salt and freshly ground black pepper.

2 In a separate frying pan or under the grill, cook the bacon until crispy.

3 Meanwhile, cut the croissants horizontally three-quarters the way through and spread with the mustard. Place the mushroom mix on the bottom halves of each croissant.

4 Top with the bacon, then scatter with the grated cheese and place in the oven until the cheese melts.

BACON SANDWICH

This makes a particularly good snack after a heavy night's drinking.

Serves 1
4 rashers smoked streaky or back
*   bacon, rindless*
25g or 1 oz pork dripping or butter
2 slices sliced white bread
freshly ground black pepper
butter, for spreading (optional)
ketchup or brown sauce

1 Fry the bacon over a medium heat with the dripping or butter until the bacon fat starts to turn golden. Turn the bacon once. Remove and keep warm.

2 Take the two slices of bread and liberally pepper one side. Place the peppered sides down into the fat in the bacon pan and cook until bread is golden.

3 If desired, butter the uncooked side of the bread. Place the bacon on the uncooked side.

4 Add the ketchup or brown sauce of your choice, then top with the other slice of bread, uncooked side down. Eat immediately.

DUBLIN CODDLE

Serves 8
1 x 1kg or 2 lb 2 oz unsmoked bacon joint,
soaked in water overnight
450g or 1 lb pork and leek sausages, browned
1kg or or 2 lb 2 oz potatoes, diced
450g or 1 lb onions, sliced
1 tsp of soft thyme leaves
½ tsp ground white pepper
½ tsp English mustard powder
4 tbsp chopped flat-leaf parsley
½ Savoy cabbage, chopped
2 bay leaves
chicken stock
55g or 2 oz unsalted butter, cut in small cubes

1 Preheat the oven to 170°C or 325°F or gas mark 3.

2 Cut the bacon joint into 5cm (2-inch) pieces. Cut the sausages into quarters.

3 Combine the potatoes, onions, thyme, pepper, mustard, parsley, cabbage and bay leaves in a bowl.

4 Make several layers using the bacon, sausage and the potato mix in a deep casserole and pour over enough stock to come level with the final layer of potatoes. Dot the surface of the coddle with the butter cubes.

5 Place the casserole over a medium heat, bring to a simmer, cover and place in the oven for about 2 hours, or until the bacon is tender.

6 If required, increase the oven temperature and remove the lid for the last 30 minutes to brown the top layer – although this drastic step would not be considered traditional in Dublin. Serve with some wedges of buttered soda bread.

3

Lamb

Buying & cooking lamb

British lamb is available from early spring from the winter-born lambs of Southern England through to the end of summer from lambs born in the Highlands of Scotland and the mountains of Wales. During autumn, lamb has much darker flesh as it progresses towards its post-Christmas name of hogget; thereafter it is mutton.

Welsh lamb is often said to be the best, but I've enjoyed some fabulous lamb with a salty flavour that comes from the wild shores of Scotland. Luckily, we can still buy lamb that has not been so intensively reared and is free from hormones and enforced protein.

I'm not a great fan of lamb sold before it has weaned (eight to ten weeks); this milk-fed lamb may be tender but it is also fairly tasteless and ridiculously priced. Buy lamb with a good coating of creamy white fat that is firm to the touch and has a rosy, pink flesh; the younger the animal, generally the paler the flesh is going to be.

Roasting

Buy a leg or half leg or a boned and rolled shoulder. The shoulder will be more fatty, but it tends to have more flavour. You can buy a rack of best end, but it is an expensive cut, producing only seven or eight cutlets.

Trim your joint of excess fat, but leave enough on to baste it during cooking. I like to spike a leg of lamb with rosemary, anchovy and garlic; left overnight and roasted in the normal way, it imparts an extra dimension to the meat and, once roasted, you will not notice any overwhelming flavour of the anchovy.

Never season the meat with salt until just prior to cooking, as the salt will draw out the blood and toughen the meat. Smear dripping or oil over the joint, then seal the meat all over in a hot pan so that the meat is golden brown.

Place the lamb is a roasting tray on a few garlic cloves, some thyme and bay leaves. De-glaze the searing pan with some red wine or stock and pour into the bottom of the roasting tray. During roasting, add more stock from time to time to the roasting pan unless you surround the lamb with potatoes. These juices will provide a good base for your gravy.

Roast the lamb in a 200°C or 400°F or gas mark 6 oven for 30 minutes, then lower to 180°C (350°F, gas mark 4) for the remaining time. Allow 12 to 15 minutes per pound for medium-rare and up to 25 minutes for well-cooked. Always allow the meat to rest after cooking for 10 to 15 minutes in a warm place to relax the fibres and distribute the delicious juices.

While the lamb is resting, pour off the surface fat from the roasting tray and de-glaze the pan with wine or stock with a splash of vinegar; add a dash each of Worcestershire sauce, anchovy essence and mushroom essence. Mash the roast garlic into the *jus* with a fork. Strain into a gravy boat after checking the seasoning. If you are a packet-gravy fan (and many are), follow the above recipe but add a teaspoonful of your favourite gravy powder. It will still taste better than just using a packet.

Grilling and frying

Fast methods of cooking demand tender cuts: noisettes, cutlets, chump chops or leg steaks. For an impressive barbecue grilling cut, ask you butcher to 'butterfly' a whole leg of lamb.

Rub the meat with oil to prevent sticking. If using an overhead grill, make sure it is turned on well ahead of time to heat up. I always think this form of grilling is messy, as the fat spits, creating a very greasy grill. In addition, often with modern grills, the heat is not powerful enough to give the meat a delicious crust.

I prefer to cheat the grilling by using a ridged griddle pan. Always season during cooking or after, as you don't want to draw out the meat's natural juices. Single chops will take seven to 10 minutes to cook, double chops or large chump chops could take 15 minutes. Seal the meat over a high heat, then reduce the temperature to finish the cooking.

Braising, stewing and pot-roasting

Use the shoulder, shank or neck chops. This is a moist, slow method of cooking, so you need to use cuts that have a good level of fat which will slowly disperse during the process.

Flour the meat and brown in oil, butter or dripping before adding vegetables, herbs, wine and stock. By the end of cooking time you should be able to carve the meat with a spoon as it slips from the bone. The flavours will have melded together. The liquid in the casserole should just come to the top of the meat. Don't be shy of using herbs such as thyme or bay, spices and whole cloves of garlic. Give the cooking as much time as possible on a very low heat.

A braise is best done in the oven, but it could be performed carefully on a simmering heat on the hob. A braise or pot roast usually uses a large cut of meat, whereas a stew uses meat that has been cut into 2.5cm to 5cm (one- to two-inch) pieces.

Poaching or boiling

A rarely used method of cookery for lamb, but if you can find a leg of mutton, then cook it slowly in vegetable-infused water until the leg is tender. Serve with caper or onion sauce. It is a delicious method of cooking, but the meat unfortunately comes out very grey, so smother it with an old-fashioned sauce.

LAMB TAGINE

Serves 4-6
1 lamb shoulder, cut into 5cm or 2-inch dice
1½ tbsp ground ginger
2 tsp freshly ground black pepper
2 tsp cinnamon
3 tsp ground turmeric
1½ tbsp paprika
1 tsp cayenne pepper
3 tbsp olive oil
1 head of garlic, peeled and crushed with salt
450g or 1 lb grated onion
175g or 6 oz dried apricots, soaked in water
85g or 3 oz flaked almonds
55g or 2 oz sultanas or raisins
1 tbsp liquid honey
1 tsp saffron stamens, soaked in cold water
600ml or 20 fl oz tomato juice
600ml or 20 fl oz lamb stock
1 x 400g or 14 oz tin tomatoes, roughly chopped

1 Preheat the oven to 170°C or 325°F or gas mark 3. Coat the lamb in half the ground spices and leave overnight.

2 In a heavy saucepan, brown the lamb in half the oil over a medium heat; do not scorch or the spices will turn bitter. Remove the meat and set aside. Add the remaining spices, crushed garlic and grated onion to the pan. Allow the onion to soften without browning.

3 Add the apricots and soaking water, the almonds, sultanas, honey, saffron, tomato juice, half the lamb stock and tomatoes. Bring to a boil, then place in the oven. Cook for 2½ to 3 hours, checking occasionally; top up stock as necessary.

4 Fry the lemon rind in the remaining olive oil for a few minutes, then fold in the chopped coriander. Spoon the sauce over the lamb.

RACK OF LAMB
WITH PISTACHIO CRUST

Serves 4

*2 x 7-bone best ends of lamb (275–350g
    each or 10–12 oz each), each cut in half*
1 tbsp mustard

For the crust
55g or 2 oz unsalted butter, melted
55g or 2 oz shelled pistachio nuts
2 tbsp fresh soft thyme leaves
2 tbsp snipped fresh chives
2 tbsp chopped flat-leaf parsley
50g or 2 oz fresh white breadcrumbs
grated rind of ½ lemon
1 small garlic clove, roughly chopped
salt and freshly ground black pepper

1 Preheat the oven to 200°C or 400°F or gas
mark 6. To make the crust, pour the butter
in a food processor with the pistachio
nuts and herbs and blitz until bright green.

Add the breadcrumbs, lemon rind, garlic and seasoning and blend again for just a few seconds, until all the ingredients are well-combined.

2 Place the racks of lamb on a chopping board and, using a pastry brush, paint the mustard over the fat side of each rack. Cover with the pistachio crust, using your hands to mould it over the lamb. Arrange the lamb, coated-side up, on a baking sheet and chill for at least 30 minutes (up to 2 hours is fine) to allow the crust to set.

3 Place the racks of lamb in a small roasting tin and roast for 15 to 25 minutes, depending on how pink you like the meat. Remove from the oven and set aside in a warm place to rest for 10 to 15 minutes. Serve with new potatoes and steamed asparagus.

SHEPHERD'S PIE WITH CHEESY CAULIFLOWER MASH

Serves 6
For the shepherd's pie
115g or 4 oz streaky bacon, diced
100–125ml or 3½–4 fl oz good olive oil
1 onion, finely diced
1 celery stick, finely diced
1 carrot, peeled and finely sliced
1 tsp soft thyme leaves
1 bay leaf
1 x 400g or 14 oz tin chopped tomatoes
1 tbsp tomato purée
1 dessertspoon anchovy essence
1 tbsp Worcestershire sauce
900g or 2 lb minced lamb
1 bottle dry red wine
850ml or 30 fl oz lamb stock
salt and freshly ground black pepper

For the cauliflower mash
1 cauliflower, cut into florets
2 free-range egg yolks
25g or 1 oz unsalted butter
85g or 3 oz freshly grated Gruyère cheese
25g or 1 oz freshly grated Parmesan cheese
salt and freshly ground black pepper

1 In a large, heavy-based saucepan, fry the bacon in 1 tablespoon of olive oil. When the bacon is crisp and has released some natural fats, add the onion, celery, carrot, thyme, and bay leaf and cook over a medium heat until the vegetables have softened and taken on a little colour.

2 Add the tinned tomatoes, tomato purée, anchovy essence and Worcestershire sauce. Stir to combine. Cook over a medium heat.

3 Meanwhile, in a large frying pan, heat a little olive oil and fry off the minced lamb in small batches, until browned. While the meat is frying, break up any lumps with the back of a wooden spoon. Repeat using a little more oil each time, if necessary, until all the meat is used up. Add each batch of meat to the sauce mix.

4 De-glaze the frying pan with some of the red wine, scraping any crusty bits from the bottom, then pour this wine, the remaining wine and the stock into the meat pot.

5 Bring to the boil, reduce the heat and simmer, stirring from time to time, for about 1 hour, until the meat is tender. Season to taste. If the liquid reduces too much, top up with water.

6 While the meat simmers, place the cauliflower florets into a pan of salted boiling water and cook until tender. Drain well and place into the bowl of a food processor. Add the egg yolks, butter, half the Gruyère cheese and half the Parmesan, then purée until smooth but with a little bit of texture. Season to taste.

7 Once the lamb is cooked, allow it to cool slightly, then spoon into the bottom of an ovenproof dish. Spoon the cauliflower mash on top, sprinkle with the remaining cheeses and bake in a 200°C or 400°F or gas mark 6 oven until hot and bubbling.

BALLYMALOE IRISH STEW

Serves 6

1.5 kg or 3 lb 5 oz lamb chops (neck or chump)
no less than 2.5 cm or 1-inch thick
2 tbsp dripping or olive oil
6 onions, peeled and cut in quarters
through the root
6 carrots, peeled and cut in 1 cm or
half-inch slices
750–900 ml or 26–32 fl oz lamb or
chicken stock (or water)
salt and freshly ground black pepper
8–12 potatoes, peeled and cut in 2.5 cm or
1-inch slices
1 tsp chopped soft thyme leaves
1 tbsp softened butter (optional)
1 tbsp flour (optional)
1 tbsp chopped flat-leaf parsley
1 tbsp snipped chives

1 Preheat the oven to 180°C or 350°F or gas mark 4. Cut the chops in half and trim off and discard any excess fat.

2 In a large, heavy-based saucepan over a low heat, melt down the dripping or oil. Place the chops in the saucepan and fry to brown all over. Remove and set aside.

3 To the saucepan add the onions and sweat them until soft but not brown. Add the carrots and cook for 2 to 3 minutes; remove and set aside. De-glaze the pan with the stock.

4 In a casserole dish, layer the lamb chops with the onions and carrots until three-quarters of the way up the casserole dish. Season each layer, then pour the de-glazed juices and stock into the casserole.

5 Lay the potatoes on top and sprinkle with the thyme. Bring to the boil. Cover with wet greaseproof paper, then the lid of the casserole. Transfer to the oven or simmer on the top of the stove for 1 to 1½ hours, or until the stew is completely cooked. Serve immediately.

6 Alternatively, once the stew is cooked, remove the cooking liquor into another pan and skim off any fat. You can thicken the sauce by making a roux with the butter and flour. Melt the butter in a small pan and stir in the flour. Cook for 3 to 4 minutes over a low heat. Stir this into the sauce little by little until you reach the desired consistency.

7 Season to taste and add the parsley and chives. Pour the sauce back into the casserole and bring back to boiling point on top of the stove. Serve straight from the pot with some crusty bread.

CRISPY LAMB

Serves 4
450g or 1 lb raw lamb from the leg,
   cut into thin strips
6 garlic cloves, mashed
1 x 5cm or 2-inch piece of fresh ginger, grated
1 tsp chilli powder
1 tbsp chopped coriander
4 tbsp Greek yoghurt
2 eggs, beaten
140g or 5 oz breadcrumbs, toasted
vegetable oil, for frying

1 Combine the lamb in a bowl with the garlic, ginger, chilli powder, coriander and yoghurt. Allow to marinade, overnight if possible.

2 Dip the lamb strips into the egg, then fold the strips into the breadcrumbs. As you coat the lamb, separate the pieces. Heat the oil in a frying pan and deep-fry in small batches, until crisp.

Lamb kebabs with Moroccan mint mechoui

Serves 8
1 leg of lamb, about 2.25kg or 5 lb,
  cut into 5cm or 2-inch cubes
6 courgettes, cut into 2.5cm
  or 1-inch chunks
6 red onions, peeled and quartered
3 tbsp olive oil

For the marinade
1 cup chopped fresh mint
juice of 2 lemons
1 tbsp finely minced garlic
2 tbsp ground coriander
1 tsp cayenne pepper
2 tsp paprika
2 tsp ground cumin
2 tsp freshly ground pepper
75ml or 2½ fl oz olive oil
2 tbsp chopped fresh mint, to garnish

1 Place the lamb in a non-aluminium container. Combine all the marinade ingredients and rub over the meat. Cover. Refrigerate overnight or let stand 2 to 3 hours at room temperature. Bring back to room temperature, if refrigerated.

2 Place the courgettes and onion in the olive oil, season with salt and freshly ground black pepper, and let stand for 15 minutes.

3 Remove the meat from the marinade. Skewer a chunk of lamb onto a pre-soaked wooden skewer, followed by a chunk of courgette, then one of red onion. Repeat until you have three pieces of lamb and vegetables on each skewer.

4 Cook until medium-rare on a barbecue or grill, about 5 minutes each side. Sprinkle with a little chopped mint before serving (optional).

Moussaka

Serves 4-6
175ml or 6 fl oz olive oil
1 large onion, finely chopped
3 garlic cloves, chopped
1 tbsp fresh thyme leaves
900g or 2 lb lamb mince
2 bay leaves
1 tbsp fresh oregano, chopped
½ tsp cinnamon
¼ tsp allspice
175ml or 6 fl oz white wine
2 x 400g or 14 oz tin chopped tomatoes
lamb stock
4 medium aubergines, cut into 1 cm or
*   half-inch slices*
salt and freshly ground black pepper
plain flour, for dusting

For the béchamel sauce
85g or 3 oz unsalted butter
85g or 3 oz plain flour
900ml or 32 fl oz milk
85g or 3 oz Parmesan cheese, grated
55g or 2 oz Gruyère, grated
freshly grated nutmeg
2 egg yolks
1 egg

1 Heat 2 tablespoons of the olive oil in a large pan. Add the onion, garlic and thyme and gently cook for 10 minutes, or until the onion is soft, but not coloured.

2 Add the mince and fry until the lamb has turned brown. Break up the meat with a wooden fork until it has a loose texture.

3 Stir in the bay leaves, oregano, cinnamon, allspice and wine and cook for 5 minutes.

4 Add the tomatoes, reduce the heat and simmer for approximately 1 hour. If the meat becomes too dry, add a little lamb stock.

5 Meanwhile, place the aubergines in a colander, sprinkle with salt and leave for 30 minutes. This draws out any bitter juices.

6 Make the béchamel sauce. Melt the butter in a non-stick pan and stir in the flour. Cook for 5 minutes before gradually stirring in the milk. Stir continuously until the sauce thickens. Simmer over a gentle heat for 8 to 10 minutes. Stir in 55g or 2 oz of the Parmesan and 25g or 1 oz of the Gruyère; season with salt and pepper. Dot the surface with butter to prevent a skin from forming and set aside.

7 Rinse the aubergines and pat dry. Dust with flour and fry in batches in the remaining olive oil until golden on both sides, about 8 to 10 minutes. Drain on kitchen paper. Set aside until ready to construct the moussaka.

8 Gently reheat the béchamel sauce and stir in the egg yolks and egg. Season with nutmeg and salt and pepper.

9 Remove the bay leaves from the mince and season with salt and pepper.

10 Cover the base of an ovenproof dish (30 x 20cm or 12 x 8 inches) with half the aubergine slices, and then spoon over half the mince. Repeat the layers and then pour on the cheese sauce. Sprinkle with the remaining Parmesan and the Gruyère.

11 Bake in a preheated oven at 180°C or 350°F or gas mark 4 for 50 to 60 minutes, or until golden and bubbling. Allow to settle for 5 minutes before cutting into squares and serving.

12 Serve the moussaka with a chunky tomato, cucumber, parsley and mint salad and some crusty bread.

Classic roast lamb with garlic, anchovies & rosemary

Serves 6
1 x 2.7kg or 6 lb leg of British lamb
1 head of garlic, split into cloves, 6 cloves
*   peeled and thinly sliced*
2 sprigs of rosemary, broken into little
*   spriglets of 4 or 5 leaves*
6 anchovies, rinsed and filleted
salt and freshly ground black pepper
dripping, lard, butter or duck fat
1 potato, peeled and sliced
1 onion, peeled and sliced
1 carrot, peeled and sliced

For the gravy
175ml or 6 fl oz light red wine
1 sprig rosemary
300ml or 10 fl oz chicken or vegetable stock
    or cooking water from the vegetables
1 dessertspoon redcurrant jelly

1 Make deep incisions with the point of a sharp knife about 2.5cm or 1 inch apart all over the lamb. Into each hole, place a sliver of garlic encased in a tuft of rosemary and held together by wrapping around a sliver of anchovy fillet. Allow the lamb to rest in the fridge overnight (or for at least 4 hours).

2 Season the lamb all over with salt and black pepper. Smear it with a fat of your choice.

3 Preheat the oven to 200°C or 400°F or gas mark 6.

4 Place the sliced vegetables in the bottom of a roasting tray with the remaining peeled garlic cloves and some more fat.

5 Put the lamb on top of the vegetables and place it in the middle of the oven. Cook for 20 minutes, then turn the oven down to 180°C or 350°F or gas mark 4. Baste the lamb with the melted fat every 20 minutes.

6 Cook for another 1 to 1½ hours, depending on how rare you enjoy your meat.

7 Remove the lamb and vegetables from the oven to rest for at least 15 minutes (this helps the juices to settle) while you are making the gravy.

8 To make the gravy, drain the fat from the roasting tray, leaving behind any juices that have exuded from the meat. Place the tray over a medium heat and pour in the red wine.

9 Bring to the boil, scraping all the grungy bits that have caramelized in the bottom of the pan. Boil for 3 to 4 minutes, then add the rosemary, stock and redcurrant jelly. Boil for a further 8 minutes.

10 Season to taste with salt and freshly ground black pepper and strain into a gravy boat. The gravy can be thickened with a little flour mixed into a paste with an equal quantity of butter, if you so desire.

11 Carve the lamb and offer some of the tasty (but by now not very attractive!) roasted vegetables that were underneath the meat. Serve the gravy separately.

SOUVLAKIA SANDWICH

A great street food from Greece, souvlakia is usually served as a kebab.

Serves 8
For the marinade
1 onion, peeled and thinly sliced
4 tbsp flat-leaf parsley
175ml or 6 fl oz extra-virgin olive oil
85ml or 3 fl oz lemon juice
2 tbsp finely chopped garlic
4 tbsp chopped oregano
1 tbsp freshly ground black pepper
¼ tsp dried chilli flakes
½ tsp ground cumin
½ tsp ground coriander
1 tsp salt

1kg or 2 lb 4 oz boneless leg of lamb, shredded
8 pitta breads
juice of ½ lemon
4 tbsp Greek yoghurt
½ tsp each chopped mint & coriander leaves
3 spring onions, thinly sliced

1 Blend all the marinade ingredients in a food processor or blender until you have a smooth purée. Pour over the lamb and mix to combine. Allow the lamb to marinade for up to four hours.

2 In a very hot, non-stick pan, fry the lamb for 2 to 3 minutes each side.

3 Warm the pitta breads; cut the edges to form a pocket. Stuff in the lamb and drizzle with the fresh lemon juice, yoghurt, fresh herbs and spring onions.

LANCASHIRE HOTPOT

Serves 4

8 x 175g or 6 oz lamb chump chops,
  excess fat removed
4 lamb's kidneys, skinned, cored and quartered
1 heaped tbsp seasoned flour
1 tbsp of dripping
85g or 3 oz unsalted butter
1.2kg or 2 lb 12 oz floury potatoes
  (King Edward or Maris Piper), peeled
  and cut into 1cm or ½-inch slices
2 onions, peeled and finely sliced
2 sprigs fresh thyme
2 bay leaves
salt and freshly ground black pepper
600ml or 20 fl oz fresh lamb stock

1 Preheat the oven to 180°C or 350°F or gas mark 4. Place the lamb and kidneys in a bowl and mix in the seasoned flour to coat the meat. Heat the dripping in a large non-stick frying pan and brown the meat in batches.

2 Butter the inside of heavy 4.5-litre or 8-pint casserole dish with 25g or 1 oz of the butter and line the bottom with a layer of potatoes. Top the potatoes with four of the chops, half the kidneys and onions, a sprig of thyme, a bay leaf and a good seasoning of salt and pepper.

3 Repeat, using the remaining lamb, kidneys, onions, thyme, and bay leaf. Season. Finish with a layer of potato slices, each slice slightly overlapping the other.

4 Pour on the stock. Melt the remaining butter and brush the potatoes with it. Cover the casserole and place in the preheated oven for 2 hours.

5 Remove the lid of the casserole and cook for a further 30 to 40 minutes, until the potatoes are golden brown and the meat is completely tender. Serve with broccoli and carrots.

CHOPPED PEPPERED LAMB

A peppered lamb burger by any other name.
Slap it between burger buns if you fancy and
serve with chips.

Serves 2-4
450g or 1 lb minced lamb (20% fat)
2 tbsp crushed black peppercorns
12 garlic cloves
1 sprig thyme
1 bay leaf
300ml or 10 fl oz water
olive oil
3 tbsp chopped mint
55g or 2 oz unsalted butter, cut into small cubes
salt and freshly ground black pepper

1 Shape the lamb into four burgers and coat them all over with the crushed peppercorns. Poach the garlic, thyme and bay leaf in the water for about 15 minutes, or until the garlic is tender. Remove the garlic and reserve; strain the liquor and keep for later.

2 In a hot frying pan with a little oil, sear the burgers with the garlic cloves for 2 minutes on each side. Lower the heat and cook for a further minute each side, depending on how rare you like your meat. Remove the burgers and the browned garlic and keep warm.

3 Pour the garlic liquor into the lamb pan (there should be about 125ml or 4 fl oz). Add the mint and butter and whisk to emulsify.

4 Put the lamb and garlic on warm plates, season and top with the sauce. Serve with a leafy salad.

5
Game

Buying & cooking game

Game used to apply to anything that wasn't bred on a farm. Our ancestors would kill and eat anything that moved – nothing was sacred: swan, peacock, thrush, blackbird, wild pig. Nowadays we are limited as to what we can kill and eat, and much of what used to be wild is now reared on farms: quail, venison, partridge, rabbit and wild (or not) boar.

While shooting is not popular with many people, you can't deny the fact that the wild bird or animal has a much better flavour than its domestic counterpart. It is all to do with what they eat; reared on real, wild food, they have had a life.

On the following pages, you will find a list most game animals that you are likely to find in the shops.

Grouse

Season: 12 August to 10 December

Possibly the UK's finest game bird, probably because it is the one bird that is native only to the British Isles. The French have always been desperate to rear grouse, but they've never succeeded – probably because the birds feed almost entirely on young heather shoots on the moors of Scotland, Ireland, Yorkshire and Derbyshire.

Buy the birds at the beginning of the season, when they are young and tender. The spur at the back of the leg should be soft and rounded. These are one-man birds, weighing approximately 500g (1 lb 2 oz). A wild bird that is such a treat should be respected by cooking it as simply as possible, roast preferably in a 200°C (400°F or gas mark 6) oven for 20 to 35 minutes, depending on how rare you enjoy it. If, perchance, you happen upon an older bird, braise it; failing that, if you have some other game hanging around, make a game pie.

Mallard or wild duck

Season: 1 September to 31 January

A perfect size for two (1–1.5kg or around 2–3lb), although the smaller widgeon and teal are really one-man birds. Wild duck should not be hung for long as it is fatter than most wild birds and the fat could turn rancid. Once plucked, it will look like a smaller version of domestic duck. As it feeds on water life, there is a chance of it being a little fishy in flavour. To safeguard against this, pop half a lemon, some thyme sprigs and half an onion into its cavity when cooking.

The flesh is dark and has a tendency toward dryness. A medium-sized bird will cook in a 200°C (400°F or gas mark 6) oven in about 30 minutes; allow 10 minutes for it to rest after roasting. You won't get much pleasure from the legs, so eat the breast, then use the carcass for soup or mince the leg meat for a sauce to accompany pasta.

Partridge

Season: 1 September to 1 February

One of my favourite game birds, as generally it is tender but not overpowering. Young birds should have soft feet and pointed flight feathers. Another one-portion bird, young ones should be roasted (25 to 35 minutes in a 200°C or 400°F or gas mark 6 oven), older birds braised with cabbage or added to casseroles, terrines or soups.

Pheasant

Season: 1 October to 1 February

One bird will produce two to four portions, depending on your appetite. Some old country folk leave pheasants to hang until the guts drop out – not for me, but a little hanging does the birds a flavour favour. You don't get much joy out of the leg meat, as it tends to be darker, tougher and very stringy, with strong sinews. Roast pheasants for 15 to 20 minutes per pound, then remove the breasts, chop up the carcasses to make soup or sauce, and remove the leg meat to make potted pheasant.

Pigeon

No closed season, so fire away

You need plump, country, wood pigeons, preferably young. Like most game birds, the breast is for eating and the legs can be potted or made into soup or meatballs. A good pigeon is surprisingly good, considering its cheap price. The breasts can be really tender especially if cooked rare and sliced thin. Roasting times: 15 to 25 minutes at 200°C (400°F or gas mark 6).

Rabbit

No closed season

Rabbit can be bought wild and farmed. Frozen rabbit is often imported from China. Rabbit can be cooked in many recipes that use chicken or veal. The rabbit saddle is often roasted, or it can be boned and stuffed. The legs can be casseroled or braised, and the forequarter meat can be minced and made into meatballs. Wild rabbit tends to be a lot tougher than farmed, but accordingly it has more flavour, and is a lot cheaper.

Venison

Season varies in England, Wales and Scotland
Can be bought wild or farmed, although most of what we buy is farmed. Venison was touted as the meat to replace our so-called 'unhealthy diet of beef', but so far it hasn't really taken off. Europe imports much of our venison, as the Continentals rate it very highly.

Buy young venison where possible and treat it much as you would beef. Grill or roast the loin or saddle and braise the legs. The forequarter can be stewed or cooked in mince form. The meat from venison is very lean, dark and dense-textured, high in protein and low in saturated fat. When roasting or braising venison, it is advisable to 'lard' the meat, which means inserting strips of pork fat into it. This is done with a larding needle.

PAPPARDELLE WITH RABBIT SAUCE

Serves 4
For the rabbit
1 medium-sized farmed rabbit
4 tbsp white-wine vinegar
2 tbsp olive oil
1 small onion, finely chopped
2 garlic cloves, halved
sprig of fresh rosemary
salt and freshly ground black pepper
150ml or 5 fl oz dry white wine

For the sauce
4 tbsp olive oil
2 garlic cloves, chopped
1 medium onion, finely chopped
2 chillies, finely sliced
2 x 400g or 14 oz tins chopped tomatoes
2 tsp tomato purée
1 bay leaf
1 bunch basil leaves
salt and freshly ground black pepper

450g or 1 lb pappardelle pasta
basil leaves, for garnish

METHOD

1 Cut the rabbit into pieces, wash them and put into a bowl. Pour on the vinegar and enough water to cover. Leave for 5 minutes and wash again. Put the rabbit in a pot of cold water, bring to the boil and cook for 5 minutes. Refresh under cold water.

2 Heat the oil in a saucepan. Add the onion, garlic and rosemary and cook for 8 minutes (without the onion colouring). Add the dried rabbit pieces and cook until the meat is browned all over, turning regularly. Add the white wine and cook until it has nearly evaporated. Remove the rabbit from the pan and set aside.

3 For the sauce, heat the oil and gently fry the garlic, onion and chillies until soft but without colour. Add the tomatoes, cover and slowly bring to the boil. Cook on a medium heat for 15 minutes.

4 Remove from the heat and press the tomato mixture through a sieve and return to the pot. Add the rabbit, purée, bay leaf and basil and season with salt and pepper. Cover; bring back to the boil for about 1 to 2 minutes. Reduce to a very low heat and cook for about 1 hour, or until the meat falls off the bone easily.

5 Remove the rabbit from the sauce; remove the meat from the bones and set aside (discard the bones). Remove the bay leaf. Return the rabbit meat to the sauce.

6 Bring a pan of boiling salted water to a rolling boil. Cook the pasta as per packet instructions until it is *al dente*. Drain and return to the pot, add the sauce and toss gently. Divide the mixture among four warmed serving plates and garnish with the fresh basil leaves.

Rabbit with fennel & chicory

A Mediterranean adaptation that imparts wonderful, earthy flavours.

Serves 4-6
4 tbsp extra-virgin olive oil
1 medium onion, finely chopped
1 tsp rosemary, chopped
1 chilli, finely diced
2 garlic cloves, finely diced
1 bay leaf
2 heads fennel, quartered
2 heads chicory, halved lengthways
1.5kg or 3 lb 5 oz tinned chopped tomatoes
2 large red peppers, roasted and peeled,
    each cut into 4
375ml or 13 fl oz chicken stock
8 rabbit saddle fillets
salt and freshly ground black pepper
2 tbsp flat-leaf parsley, coarsely chopped
1 tbsp basil, chopped
1 tbsp black olives, chopped

1 Heat two tablespoons of the olive oil in a saucepan over a low heat. Fry the onion, rosemary, chilli, garlic and bay leaf until the onions are soft and translucent. Add the fennel, chicory and tomatoes. Cover and simmer gently for about 35 minutes, or until the fennel has cooked.

2 Add the peppers and half the stock. Increase the heat to reduce the sauce by half. Reserve.

3 Trim the rabbit fillets of any fat or silver skin. Season with salt and pepper. Cook in the rest of the olive oil for 5 to 8 minutes, until brown on all sides.

4 Transfer the rabbit to the vegetable stew. Add a little more stock, if needed; simmer to reheat. Slice the fillets onto serving plates; spoon around the vegetables. Sprinkle with parsley, basil and olives. Serve with new potatoes.

VENISON CHILLI
FOR A CROWD

If venison mince is hard to find, you can substitute a mixture of coarsely ground pork or beef.

Serves 8-12
For the chilli crème fraîche
2 cloves garlic, mashed with ½ tsp sea salt
1 tsp chilli powder
½ tsp ground cumin
3 tbsp lime juice
3 tbsp chopped coriander
3 tbsp chopped parsley
350g or 12 oz crème fraîche or sour cream

For the venison chilli
55g or 2 oz lard or 2 tbsp olive oil
2kg or 4 lb 8 oz venison, coarsely ground
1kg or 2 lb 4 oz onions, finely diced
3 sticks celery

1 tbsp garlic, finely diced
4 chillies, finely diced
500g or 1 lb 2 oz streaky bacon,
1 bay leaf
2 tbsp each cumin and oregano
1 tbsp powdered coriander
1½ tbsp paprika
1 tbsp fennel seed
1 tbsp cayenne pepper
1 tbsp unsweetened cocoa powder
1 tsp ground cinnamon
1 tbsp freshly ground black pepper
2 x 400g or 14 oz tins chopped tomatoes
beef stock as required
2 tbsp tomato purée
handful of coriander leaves, to fold in
      if desired
2 x 400g or 14 oz tins red kidney beans,
      drained and rinsed

METHOD

1 The day before you intend serving the chilli, make the chilli crème fraîche by combining all its ingredients. Refrigerate overnight. This will keep for three days in the fridge.

2 To make the chilli, heat the lard or oil in a large saucepan. Brown the ground venison in it, working in batches if necessary. Remove and set aside.

3 In the same pan, cook the onion, celery garlic, and chillies in the fat until golden brown. Cut the streaky bacon into 1cm or half-inch cubes and add it to the mix, along with the bay leaf, oregano and spices. Brown.

4 Return the meat to the pan and add all other ingredients except the kidney beans and the coriander.

5 Simmer for 2 hours. Add the beans; cook for a further half hour, fold in the coriander leaves and season to taste. Serve with chilli crème fraîche.

MEDALLIONS OF VENISON
WITH REDCURRANTS

Serves 4
12 medallions of venison loin, about 40g or
*   1½ oz each*
salt and freshly ground black pepper
1 tbsp olive oil
25g or 1 oz unsalted butter

For the sauce
1 wine glass of red wine
2 tbsp red-wine vinegar
300ml or 10 fl oz good venison or beef stock
1 tbsp redcurrant jelly
1 bay leaf
3 peppercorns
4 tbsp fresh or frozen redcurrants
*   (if frozen, defrost and sprinkle with sugar)*

1 Season the venison with salt and freshly ground black pepper. Heat the oil and butter in a heavy-based frying pan over a high heat

and sear the medallions for 1 minute on each side. Remove, set aside and keep warm.

2 To make the sauce, remove the excess fat from the frying pan, then return the pan to the heat. Pour in the wine and the wine vinegar. Turn up the heat and, stirring briskly with a wooden spoon, scrape the base and sides of the pan to release the coagulated meat juices.

3 Bring the liquid to a boil. Stir in the stock, redcurrant jelly, bay leaf and peppercorns. Bring back to a boil and allow to reduce to a light coating consistency. Add the redcurrants to the sauce and heat through for a few seconds. Adjust the seasoning to taste.

4 To serve, place three medallions on each serving plate, pour on the sauce and serve with braised red cabbage.

Tea-smoked quail with baby lettuce and Asian dressing

Serves 4 as a starter, 2 as a main course
4 x quail
sesame oil
3 large handfuls baby lettuce leaves
1 bunch small, thin asparagus

For the smoking mixture
2 tbsp each jasmine tea, brown sugar
    & long-grain rice, mixed together

For the dressing
2 garlic cloves, finely chopped
1 tbsp each chopped mint & basil leaves
2 tbsp chopped coriander
3 tbsp sunflower oil
3 tbsp fresh lime juice
2 tbsp soft brown sugar
1½ tbsp Thai fish sauce (nam pla)
1 tsp sweet chilli sauce

1 Preheat the oven to 200°C or 400°F or gas mark 6. Rub each quail with a little sesame oil; put on a rack that will fit in a wok with a lid. Cut out a small (20cm or 8-inch) circle of aluminium foil. Fold it into a container about 12cm (4½ inches) in diameter. Pour the tea-smoking mixture into this and place it in the bottom of the wok. Turn the heat to full. Once the tea starts smoking, add the rack with the quail. Cover and leave for 8 minutes.

2 Remove from the heat; don't lift the lid. Let rest for 5 minutes to allow the smoke to dissipate. When cool, remove the quail; put in a preheated oven for 2 to 3 minutes.

3 Combine all dressing ingredients and allow the flavours to develop for half an hour.

4 Blanch the asparagus in boiling salted water for 3 minutes; plunge into ice-water. Cut into 2.5cm (1-inch) pieces. Combine with the lettuce. Toss with the dressing. Cut the quail into small pieces. Serve on the dressed leaves.

ROAST PARTRIDGE WITH
SAUSAGE STUFFING

Serves 4
For the stuffing
1 red onion, finely chopped
4 garlic cloves, finely chopped
2 stalks celery, finely chopped
1 carrot, finely chopped
½ tsp fennel seeds
½ tsp soft thyme leaves
3 tbsp good olive oil
350g or 12 oz pork sausage meat
12 sage leaves
125g or 4 oz chicken livers, diced
225ml or 8 fl oz dry red wine
salt and freshly ground black pepper
85g or 3 oz soft white breadcrumbs

For the birds
4 partridge
4 slices Parma ham
olive oil
3 garlic cloves, finely chopped
1 onion, finely diced
1 tsp soft thyme leaves
125g or 4 oz chicken
    livers, chopped
55g or 2 oz dried cep or porcini mushrooms,
    soaked for ½ hour, drained, squeezed
    and chopped (reserve the soaking liquor)
350ml or 12 fl oz dry red wine
25g or 1 oz unsalted butter
salt and freshly ground black pepper

METHOD

1 To make the stuffing, in a large saucepan cook the onion, garlic, celery, carrot, fennel seeds and thyme in the oil until soft but not brown. Crumble the sausage meat into the onion mixture, along with the sage, and fry for 10 minutes.

2 Add the chicken livers and cook for a further 2 minutes. Add the wine and boil to reduce by half. Season with the salt and pepper, allow to cool, then fold in adequate breadcrumbs to bind.

3 Stuff the birds, then wrap each in a slice of Parma ham.

4 Heat some olive oil in a saucepan and cook the garlic, onion, thyme, chicken livers and chopped dried mushrooms until the onion is softening. Add the mushroom juices and cook until only four tablespoons of liquid remain.

5 Preheat the oven to its hottest setting. In a roasting pan, heat a little olive oil and brown the birds on each side. Roast in the oven for 10 minutes, then turn them and roast for another 10 minutes.

6 Remove the birds and keep warm. Stir the mushrooms and strained soaking liquid into the roasting pan.

7 Add the wine, scraping the bottom of the pan, and cook until the liquid has reduced by half. Add the butter and boil until emulsified. Season to taste. Serve the birds with the sauce.

SLOW HONEY-ROAST DUCK WITH A RICH ORANGE SAUCE

Serves 2-4
2.2kg or about 4 lb 8 oz Gressingham duck
1 large orange, cut into wedges
1 tsp crushed peppercorns
1 dessertspoon sea salt
3 tbsp clear honey
2 tbsp light muscovado sugar
1 tbsp Dijon mustard

For the sauce
1 large navel orange, peeled, with the peel cut
into fine strips
125ml or 4 fl oz port or Madeira
75ml or 2½ fl oz red wine vinegar
450ml or 16 fl oz fresh chicken stock
1 tsp arrowroot mixed with 1 tbsp port
or Madeira
3 tbsp Cointreau or Grand Marnier (optional)

1 Remove the excess fat from the duck's cavity. Hold the duck by the legs over a sink and pour boiling water over it three times, resting 1 minute between each pouring. Place on a rack and leave in the fridge overnight, uncovered, to dry out.

2 Preheat the oven to 220°C or 425°F or gas mark 7. Place the duck and the orange wedges into a medium roasting tin. Rub the crushed peppercorns and salt into the skin of the duck.

3 In a small bowl, mix together the honey, sugar and mustard until you have a smooth paste. Brush liberally all over the duck. Transfer to the oven and immediately reduce the heat to 170°C or 325°F or gas mark 3.

4 Cook the duck for 2¼ to 2½ hours, basting with the honey paste and duck juices every 15 minutes. Add a splash of chicken stock from time to time to prevent the honey from burning.

5 While the duck is roasting, prepare the orange sauce. Place the prepared orange strips into a small saucepan, cover with plenty of water and bring to the boil. Reduce the heat and allow to simmer for 15 minutes. Drain, pat dry with paper towels and set aside.

6 Remove the duck from the oven, cover with foil and allow to rest for 15 minutes. Carefully pour off any excess fat from the roasting tray.

7 Place the roasting tray over a high heat. Add the port or Madeira and vinegar, scraping up the roasting juices and reducing the liquid to 2 or 3 tablespoons. Pour in the remaining stock and allow to simmer for 1 minute, stirring continuously to dissolve the caramelized juices.

8 Stir in the arrowroot mixture and Cointreau or Grand Marnier (if using) and simmer for 3 to 4 minutes, or until the sauce is slightly thickened.

9 Strain the sauce into a small saucepan. Stir in the orange-peel strips and adjust the seasoning to taste. Sprinkle a little chopped parsley over the top and serve the duck, carved, with new potatoes seasoned with rock salt and wilted spinach.

WARM WOODLAND SALAD WITH PIGEON & WILD MUSHROOMS

Serves 4
2 tbsp olive oil
5 tbsp walnut oil
1 tbsp bacon lardons
3 tbsp croutons
salt and white pepper
4 pigeon breasts
85g or 3 oz unsalted butter
1 shallot, chopped
1 garlic clove, chopped
4 oyster mushrooms
1 bag mixed salad leaves

1 Preheat the oven to 200°C or 400°F or gas mark 6. Heat the walnut and olive oils in a frying pan; add the lardons. Cook until they crisp up, then add the croutons and fry until golden brown. Set aside to keep warm.

2 Season the pigeon breasts. Brown them on both sides in 25g (1 oz) of the butter, then roast them in the oven for 6 minutes. Allow to rest briefly, then carve into thin strips.

3 Sweat the shallots and garlic in the remaining butter until soft but not brown. Add the oyster mushrooms, raise the heat and sauté quickly for 1 minute each side. Season to taste. Drain the mixture and keep warm.

4 Divide the salad leaves among four warm plates. Sprinkle with lardons and croutons, and top with pigeon strips and oyster mushrooms.

Index